"*Finding Your Way* is a must read for those searching for the right path in life. Age does not matter. Reading this book is like cleaning a mirror. The more you read the clearer the image. This book might be your wake up call to get you re-energized and back into the game. It did me!"
- **Ron Wallace** - former President of UPS International

"What do I want to do with my life?" is a question we've all pondered at one time or another. If you need help coming up with the answer, you ought to read *Finding Your Way*. In this engaging parable, you'll discover four steps that will help you work through this major life decision. No matter what your age, Dan Webster and Randy Gravitt have the know-how—and the heart—to get you moving in the right direction."
- **Ken Blanchard** - coauthor of The One Minute Manager®
and Great Leaders Grow

"Everyone, regardless of age or status, wants to know that...their life and contributions to the world matter..." Here is a deeply engaging story told by two authors who, for many years, have helped countless people, young and old, find the sweet spot where their gifts meet the world's needs. May "Finding Your Way" be read by many people in many stages of life. For individual readers and the communities to which they belong, this is a book that can make a big difference."
- **Parker J. Palmer** - author of "Let Your Life Speak,"
"The Courage to Teach," and "Healing the Heart of Democracy"

"I read this book on my way out to the mountains of Colorado for the All-Star break. When I finished I realized I could have used this book about 35 years ago. A very powerful and insightful read into self discovery, purpose and peace. We've all had a crossroads experience, or four, in our lives, and this book meets the challenge head on with four themes for guidance, direction and discovery. The Johnson family is real - as are their family challenges. The help they find along the way in the Clarke family is priceless. The four themes laid out for us in the book give us a road map to follow to find our way when we get 'a little' lost."
- **Clint Hurdle** - Manager of the Pittsburg Pirates -
2013 National League Manager of the Year

"Finding Your Way is a delightful story filled with profound truths that can actually alter the trajectory of a person's life. As a mom, leader in the church, and coach of leaders, I highly endorse this incredibly valuable tool. I long for every person I come across to be fully alive, with eyes that shine whenever they get to do what they were born to do. Webster and Gravitt have created a tool that will contribute in remarkable ways to helping people find their pathway in God's kingdom."

- **Nancy Beach** - Author, Creative Consultant

"Dan and Randy's approach is incredibly practical and helpful. I followed the steps they laid out, and I discovered several new and exciting ideas for my future."

- **Austin Schulenburg** - Student

"I am a technology expert professionally, a father of two sons and the leader of a small group of ten high school seniors at my church. I recently completed working through the *Finding Your Way* process with all ten guys. Dan and Randy's approach to helping students find their way in life is ingenious. By the final step in the four step process each guy had a great idea of who they are and what could be interesting for them as they continue their schooling. Each of them walked away with confidence about their college and career choice, and were very excited about their future. About half the group changed their original plans to follow what they learned in *Finding Your Way*. I had a number of the students tell me that this should be taught as a class in High School or at least the Guidance Counselor should be able to walk them through this process."

- **Terry Schulenburg** - Technology Expert, Father and Small Group Leader

"Freedom and Confidence are what I felt after working through the *Finding Your Way* steps. I wish my school counselor knew some of this. I am ready to start working."

- **Andrew Archer** - College Freshman

"*Finding your Way* is not just an engaging story, it is a brilliant process that will help you find the work you were born to do...at any age. I'm not only giving this book to college graduates, I'm also giving it to a few fifty year old friends searching for their passion and purpose."
  - **Jon Gordon** - Best Selling Author & Keynote Speaker

"I have taught at Pennsylvania State University, Benedictine University, the University of Alberta and currently lecture for the Boler School of Business at John Carroll University. I have been involved with students for the last fifteen years as professor and mentor offering advice and support regarding choice of majors and interests. I wish I would have had a resource all these years like *"Finding Your Way."* This fable encourages reflection and assessment without categorizing what you could/should do. It also doesn't declare you "a detailed oriented person" or "a creative." Rather it empowers the reader to assess themselves AND gives them the tools to do so. There is great value in having a simple and clear organizational structure that is built into a story. I would never hand one of my students a survey or 200 pages if they came to me; but I would hand them this book."
  - **Kerrie Aman Carfagno** - Boler School of Business, John Carroll Univ

"*Finding Your Way* does a great job of clearly laying out helpful steps one might use to effectively determine a career path. Definitely a great read for anyone serious about discovering a career path where their gifts and talents will be maximized."
  - **Todd Gongwer** - author of *Lead for God's Sake*

"As a High School Senior, I was able to relate to Mark's story. I have had these conversations with my parents and had many fights break out because of how differently we look at this process. *Finding Your Way* helped me better understand who I am and what might be an interesting career choice as I head into College. I am very excited about the adventure ahead, and my parents have a better grasp on what I want to do."
  - **Matthew French** - High School Senior

"Wow! What can I say about *Finding Your Way*? Being a career and talent management expert I can say that it is the only book that I am aware of that captures a complex life altering experience with simplicity in an easy to read style. I was hooked by page four as the story reflected how I supported my sophomore college son when 'we' selected and mapped his career. I can't wait to give him this wonderful book that will assist him in not only finding his way, but will create unlimited possibilities and a world of opportunities. *Finding Your Way* is a must read for career practitioners, and should be a part of every high school reading list and placed in every college career office or provided in student enrollment packets."

    - **Indigo Debra Triplett** - Author and CEO - Careers In Transition, Inc.

"Randy and Dan are leaders – they are communicators and difference makers! Throughout their careers, they have devoted themselves to helping men and women reach their full potential. ***Finding Your Way*** is the next step in their widening circle of influence."

    - **Mark Miller** - VP of Organizational Effectiveness for the Chick-fil-A Corporation & co-author with Ken Blanchard of The Secret

"Beware! Once you start reading this book you won't be able to put it down. I finished in one sitting - so clear your calendar. When it comes to discovering your purpose, Dan and Randy nail it! *Finding Your Way* is a powerful resource that every student MUST read."

    - **Dan Britton** - Executive Vice Pres, Fellowship of Christian Athletes

"I have been planning on going to college to be an accountant since I started High School. After following the 4 steps in *Finding Your Way*, I learned that I would have been very disappointed by taking that step. I have a new outlook for my future."

    - **Sean Taylor** - High School student

FINDING YOUR WAY

FINDING YOUR WAY

DISCOVERING THE TRUTH ABOUT YOU

DAN WEBSTER &
RANDY GRAVITT

FYW Publishing LLC

Finding Your Way
Copyright 2013 © by Dan Webster and Randy Gravitt

ORDERING INFORMATION
FYW Publishing LLC
550 Old Orchard Road
Holland, MI   49423
Tel: 616-335-8500
www.findingyourway.us

Library of Congress Cataloging-in-Publication Data

Webster, Dan & Gravitt, Randy.
        Finding Your Way, discovering the truth about you
        Includes biographical references.

        ISBN   978-0-9858896-0-9

        1. Self-Leadership. 2. Self-Discovery. 3. Vocation. 4. Goals (Psychology).
        5. Spiritual Growth

Scripture quotation (Psalm 139 reference) is taken from the Holy Bible, New Living Translation, copyright ©1996, 2004, 2007 by Tyndale House Foundation. Used by permission of Tyndale House Publishers, Inc., Carol Stream, Illinois 60188. All rights reserved.

Second Edition

Design work by Troy Murphy. Troy is a brilliant creative solutionist who can be contacted at troy@launch137.com.

Dedication

Tom Paterson and Parker J. Palmer are the only sages I have had the privilege of knowing personally. Each, in his own manner, has helped me find my way. Tom is a strategic thinking guru and has helped me see that everything happens in process. Hence, *Finding Your Way*, is a process. Parker has imparted to me the importance of listening to my life and following what it tells me. Because of this, *Finding Your Way* points it's readers to have the confidence to listen closely and trust what one's life is telling them. Both Tom and Parker are relentlessly courageous in challenging others to have the belief to live the life they were meant to live. For each of their immense intellects and deep humility I thank them and dedicate this project.

- Dan Webster, March 2014

●

There is an old saying, "Those who drink the water, should never forget those who dug the well." Countless men and women have served as "well diggers" to help me find my own way, but one stands out. My co-author, Dan Webster. Dan has served as a mentor, coach, and friend to me, and it was he who first taught me that all great work begins with being authentic and flows out of the "well" of the heart. Countless people have benefitted from Dan's life and leadership, but perhaps no one has been encouraged by him more than I have. When he believed in me enough to invite me to write *Finding Your Way* with him, I was humbled and grateful. For his contribution to my own story and for serving as my Jim Clarke, I gratefully dedicate *Finding Your Way*.

- Randy Gravitt, March 2014

Contents

The Conversation - 15

The Drive Back - 19

The Wake Up - 21

Caramel Latte - 25

Lemonade - 32

The List - 37

Cartoons and Cathedrals - 39

Uncle Chuck - 42

Calling Home - 44

Frequencies - 50

Think Time - 59

Pizza - 64

Talking to Mom - 70

Rev - 76

First National Bank - 86

Regents - 94

An Outrageous Opportunity - 102

The Call - 108

One Last Latte - 110

Mark's Letter - 114

Graduation - 116

Epilogue - 118

Next Steps - 120

Finding Your Way *JOURNAL* - 125-183

About the Authors - 184

Acknowledgements - 186

Additional Resources - 188

Bring *Finding Your Way* To Your Community - 192

DISCOVERING THE TRUTH ABOUT YOU

The Conversation

"Dad, we need to talk." As the words rolled off of Mark Johnson's tongue he realized his timing could not have been worse.

It was Christmas Eve, and Mark's mom, Anne, had just removed a turkey with all the trimmings from the oven. Christmas Eve dinner was a tradition in the Johnson household. Mark's older brother and his new girlfriend had flown across the country for this special weekend. The two of them were in the kitchen with Anne, while Mark's dad, George, was hastily looking for his carving knives which he kept stashed in an antique china cabinet.

"About what?" George replied to his son with a puzzled look on his face.

Mark, who was home for Christmas break from his University, said, "It's about my major, Dad."

"What about your major?" George said as he gave Mark a stern glance.

Mustering up all of the courage he could, Mark blurted out, "I think I may be in the wrong field."

"You think you may be what?" George said, raising his voice.

"I think I may have chosen the wrong major," came

Mark's reply. "I mean, I don't know. It's just that, well, finance is not my thing anymore."

"Are you serious?" George responded with a semi-shout. "You are a senior, one semester away from graduation. Seniors don't change their majors. Son, we talked about this a couple of years ago. Remember? We decided that a finance degree would give you the best foundation to pursue a career in financial planning. You couple that with an M.B.A. and you are on your way."

"No, you decided. Remember?" Mark responded raising his own voice.

"Mark, we both discussed this at the end of your sophomore year when I got you the courier job at the bank."

"What's going on in here?" Anne asked as she walked in from the kitchen having picked up on the discussion.

"It's my mind, not yours. And no, it is not too late. It is never too late to have courage."

George said, "Guess who suddenly has decided to change his major in the middle of his senior year? . . . Your son here, who says that finances are no longer his thing." Turning to Mark, George continued, "Not your thing, huh, Mark? Well, you have certainly had no problem making them your thing every time you have cashed those big fat tuition checks I have been writing for the past four years!"

"Is this true Mark? Are you unhappy in your major?" Anne asked.

"Yes it's true!" George butted in. "He wants to do something else. I'm sure he's about to tell us he wants to play with pencils and doodle. Or maybe build model airplanes or construct something with Lincoln Logs." Looking back to Mark, George shouted, "Have you lost your mind? You are five months away from graduation. It is a little late to be changing our mind, don't you think?"

Lowering the tone, Mark once again reminded his dad, "It's my mind, not yours. And no, it is not too late. It is never too late to have courage. But I guess that is something you wouldn't understand!"

George, now mad, snapped at his son, "What is that supposed to mean?"

"You know what it means!"

Anne, recognizing the weight of the conversation and now becoming emotionally involved herself said, "Look guys, let's discuss this after we have a nice dinner. We will figure this out together."

George shouted one last time, "There is nothing to figure out. The decision has been made. Mark is going to go back and finish that degree and prepare for graduate school!"

With that, what had promised to be a memorable Christmas holiday became a nightmare. Mark could not take any more of his dad.

He said, "I'll go back all right," and up the stairs he

stormed. Within minutes he had thrown his clothes into his duffle and was out the door headed back on the three-hour drive toward campus.

The Drive Back

As Mark merged onto the turnpike, he settled in for two hundred miles of traffic-free smooth sailing. *Everyone else must be gathered around a table with their family, which is where I should be,* he thought to himself. But his pride would not allow him to turn back.

In his heart, Mark believed his life could somehow flow like the freeway, but he had no idea how to make that happen.

Looking back, he knew he had failed to be assertive when he and his dad had originally discussed the choice of a major. Had he spoken up then, maybe things would be different now.

Mark turned on the radio hoping to escape from all that was racing through his mind. But it was no use. Forty-five minutes of Christmas carols was all he could take. The songs only served to remind him of his childhood and of the fact that his parents really had tried to help him all along the way.

As a kid, Mark and his brother had spent Christmas Eve at his grandparents' house while George and Anne spent the evening at home putting together bikes and train sets for the boys. Mark's grandmother would make cookies, while Mark and his grandfather spent time tinkering in his grandfather's workshop. Mark imagined how fun it would be to be a toy maker or even a toy designer. He was really good with his hands and always loved to design things.

After a couple of hours in the shop, the cookies hit the spot, always with these same songs playing in the background.

Mark's thoughts came back to reality and the sudden realization that he was headed into a future he was not looking forward to. Not only that, classes were still two weeks away and the campus would be dead, with only a few international students still around because they lived too far away to travel home for the break. He turned off the radio and spent the last hour in silence.

As Mark pulled into the deserted lot next to his dorm where he was an RA for freshmen guys, he suddenly felt like an idiot. Realizing the dorms were closed down and the campus was a ghost town, he thought, *How could I be so stupid? I don't even have a place to stay.*

The night was cold as Mark crawled into the back seat of his old *Honda*. Thankfully, he had a blanket and a pillow. As he dozed off, he felt totally lost.

If only someone could help me find my way raced through his mind. It was the longest night of his life.

The Wake Up

Mark spent Christmas morning by himself. Thankfully, he did find a place to stay. One of the guys on his intramural soccer team lived in an apartment complex adjacent to campus, and he had left a key under the mat. The guy had flown to Oregon and had no problem allowing Mark to keep an eye on the place while crashing on the sofa. It was not ideal, but it sure beat the back seat of his *Civic*.

After grabbing a quick shower, Mark felt very alone. By mid afternoon, feeling a bit stir crazy, he decided to take a drive off campus to see if he could find some food. Four blocks from the apartment complex Mark noticed the *Open* sign flashing in the window of *The Wake Up*. When school was in session, *The Wake*, as it was referred to by the locals, was jammed every morning with students, professors, and commuters looking to start the day with supposedly the best cup of coffee in town. Somehow Mark, who was not a coffee drinker, had never visited *The Wake* during his years at the University.

That has to be a mistake. It's five minutes to four on Christmas Day. How can this place be open? Noticing four cars in the tiny parking lot, he pulled in to check it out. As he entered, he was shocked to see the place half full. He was also surprised to see Katie Clarke behind the counter. Katie and Mark shared the same finance major and occasionally studied together and chatted before classes. She welcomed him with a smile.

"What are you doing back in town?" Katie asked. "I thought you were going home for the holidays."

"Yeah, let's just say, Christmas Eve was no *Silent Night* for my family."

"What happened?" Katie probed.

"A conversation with my dad went south and rather than ruin Christmas for everybody, I decided I would head back here early."

"Must have been a pretty big argument. What could be bad enough to ruin Christmas?" Katie asked.

"My major."

"Your major? What do you mean your major?"

"Well, I have been having an increasing sense that finance is not my thing." Mark told her.

"And your dad isn't thrilled about that since it's your senior year," Katie said, stating the obvious.

"You could say that."

"Katie," Mark continued, "Can I ask you something?"

"Sure."

"You are a finance major. Are you excited about it?" Mark asked.

"Oh my gosh. I love it! I love everything about finance. I started a savings account when I was three and made my first stock purchase at age sixteen. My dad noticed this interest in me from when I was a little girl. He often kids me that my first two spoken words were *Dow Jones.*" They both laughed.

Katie kept going, "Truthfully, my dad has been on a quest to help me sort myself out my entire life. I don't know how many conversations we have had over the years about my life and what most interests me. At various times when I was in high school, he would invite his friends over to dinner. They had all sorts of different careers and he would ask them to tell me about their work. Hands down, those who had jobs in the finance area were my favorite conversations. He saw my interest early on, and when I was fifteen he introduced me to the president of our local bank. She took me to lunch and let me ask her questions for two solid hours. I think my dad must have some kind of gift when it comes to helping people discover what they are born to do. He is the one you need to be talking to," Katie finished.

"Sounds like some kind of guru instead of a dad. Maybe I will meet him sometime," Mark said.

"Well, he's coming to help me close and give me a ride home for Christmas dinner, so why don't you hang around for a couple minutes?"

No sooner had Katie spoken those words than the front door opened and in walked Jim Clarke, Katie's dad, the owner and chief barista of *The Wake Up.*

"Hey Dad. I was just talking about you. I want to introduce you to Mark Johnson. He's a fellow finance major and could use a little help with a problem he's facing."

"It is a pleasure to meet you Mark," Jim offered as he reached out his hand.

Shaking Jim's hand, Mark responded, "It is nice to meet you, too, Mr. Clarke."

Over the next couple of minutes Katie gave her dad the *Reader's Digest* of what was up with Mark, his dad, and his frustration with his finance major.

Jim told Mark that he would love to talk with him but Katie's mom was about to take a ham out of the oven and they were on a tight schedule to get home for Christmas dinner.

"Why don't you join us?" Katie invited. "You have nowhere else to go, do you?"

"That's okay. I actually need some time to clear my head," Mark declined.

"How about coming by next week for a chat, Mark?" asked Jim. "Maybe Tuesday morning at 10:00 a.m.?"

Mark, thinking to himself, *What do I have to lose?* agreed to the meeting. Little did he know it, but Mark Johnson was about to become a coffee drinker.

Caramel Latte

By the time Tuesday morning rolled around, Mark was feeling despair. His mom had tried calling him every day for the past four days, but he had refused to answer. Mark knew if he picked up the phone his mom would talk him into coming back home. That would mean facing his father and Mark just couldn't handle any more of the 'lectures' about careers and opportunities and ambition.

As he finished his second bowl of *Honey Nut Cheerios* and the 8:00 a.m. *SportsCenter* ended, his mind turned to his scheduled meeting with Jim Clarke. *What was I thinking when I agreed to this? How could some old guy possibly help me? This meeting is a waste of time.* All thoughts that caused Mark to consider blowing off the meeting.

He threw on a sweatshirt and a clean pair of jeans and decided to walk over toward *The Wake*. The four blocks would give him the opportunity to decide whether to go in or not. When he arrived at *The Wake* the place was crowded. Mark grabbed the door handle, *What the heck?*

As he walked in, he noticed there were a of couple tables near the door that were empty. He grabbed the first one he came to thinking, *I still have fifteen minutes to change my mind and ditch this idea.* But within the first minute Jim

Clarke, who was behind the counter making specialty coffees, caught Mark's eye, and there would be no turning back.

Jim gave Mark a wave and raising his index finger he mouthed, "I will be with you in about five minutes." Mark nodded back and sat there wishing he had said no to this meeting.

Within a couple of minutes Jim was finished making his last cappuccino and he walked over to where Mark was sitting.

"Good morning Mark, can I get you something to drink. It's on the house."

"I'm not much of a coffee drinker."

"Hang on one second." Jim replied before walking back behind the counter and pushing a button on what looked like a big steam machine, making a drink. Within a minute he poured a cup of the concoction and handed it to Mark who was now standing at the counter.

"Here, try this. It's a caramel latte."

"Thanks. I'll give it a shot."

"Come on back and let me show you around," Jim invited.

For the next ten minutes, Jim gave Mark the grand tour of *The Wake*. He took Mark behind the counter and showed him the *espresso* machines and the different blends of coffee. "Coffee comes in many different flavors, Mark, just like people," Jim stated with almost a hint of appreciation in his voice.

Next Jim took Mark through a door over in the corner that

Mark had not noticed. "This is one of my favorite parts of the place, Mark," Jim said, as they walked through the door. Inside was a back room where Jim stored most of his products and supplies. On the back wall of the storeroom was a French door leading to a smaller room where Jim had an office.

The office was set up with a comfortable chair and a reading lamp, and was full of books on everything from business to culture. "This is where I like to hang out when things get slow out front," Jim said.

"Very cool room," Mark commented as he finished off the latte.

As they completed the tour the two headed back out front and sat down in two leather chairs by *The Wake's* fireplace.

"So tell me what's going on with you these days Mark," Jim said, as if he and Mark had been friends for years, but had not seen each other for a couple of months.

Mark said, "Okay, but first can I ask you something that has been on my mind for the past few days?"

"Sure," said Jim.

"How come you guys were open on Christmas Day? I was surprised when I saw the *Open* sign."

Jim replied, "Good question, Mark. Years ago when I opened *The Wake* I wanted it to be a place where people would hang out as much as I wanted it to be a place where people would drink coffee. I designed the place with that in mind, built the fireplace, put in the comfortable chairs, and installed Wi-Fi before anyone else in town. I made it a place for people to make connections, because people need to be connected."

Jim continued, "As for Christmas, I knew that while it is a great time of connection with family and friends for many, for others it is the loneliest time of the year. I figured I could change that for a few people, so I decided to open for a few hours on Christmas Day in the afternoon. Katie has run the place herself the past couple of years. She says it makes her feel *Christmasy*. It is one of the only times each year I can get her in this place."

"Speaking of Katie, she tells me your Christmas holidays didn't go so well this year. Want to tell me about that?" Jim inquired.

"Well," Mark started, "My dad and I had a little disagreement."

"Little disagreements don't usually ruin Christmas," Jim replied.

"I guess, if I were being honest, it's been boiling for a few years," Mark came back. "My dad and I just don't agree on my future. It's a long story."

"I see," said Jim. "Well, I have some time if you want to tell me about it. It is up to you, Mark." The way Jim said *Mark* made Mark feel as if Jim really cared and wanted to hear his story. As if Jim were listening.

So Mark decided to download his story. For the next hour he told Jim about how he felt as if he were in the wrong major. About how his dad was the one who pushed him toward a career in finance. He told him about the fight on Christmas Eve and how his dad had made him feel guilty about all of the tuition checks. About all the stress he was feeling toward his upcoming interviews with accounting firms and possible grad schools. The unanswered phone calls from his mom and how he felt like he could never live up to his parent's expectations. Mark finished his confession by questioning whether he even wanted to finish his degree. Clearly the whole situation was torturing him.

Jim never interrupted. He just listened. When Mark was finished Jim simply nodded and with a slight wrinkle in his forehead said, "That is heavy stuff, Mark."

After a few seconds of silence, Jim probed, "Do you know what you want your future to look like, Mark?"

Mark responded, "No. Not really."

Mark finished his confession by questioning whether he even wanted to finish his degree. Clearly the whole situation was torturing him.

Jim said, "Well, I'll tell you what. I would be willing to meet with you one on one, once a month, between now and graduation to see if we can help you sort yourself out. There are a couple of things I ask, though. First, you must be committed to the process of discovery. If you are willing to do the work, I am confident you can find your way. Next, there are a few things I will ask you to do along the way. You might say homework assignments. They will not take a lot of time, but they will require a little work. The exercises will help you get to where you want to go, even though you have no idea where that is right now," Jim finished with a slight smile on his face.

"So, what do you say, Mark? You pick the time of day based on your class schedule and I will pick the places."

It sounded a little too good to be true to Mark, but he reluctantly agreed. "Fridays work best with my class load this semester," Mark said.

"Then Fridays it is," agreed Jim. "Let's make it the first Friday of each month at this same time, 10:00 a.m. We will start ten days from today at 721 Sunset Drive. Meet me there, dress warmly, and don't be late."

Mark said, "I'll be there."

The Finding Your Way Process

Step One

LOOK BACK

Lemonade

The next ten days seemed to crawl. But with classes about to start back the campus began to show some signs of life. During the week leading up to the meeting Mark spent a lot of time thinking about his future, but the more he thought about it, the more hopeless he felt. He did manage to take a call from his mom on Tuesday evening, but when she asked him to speak to his dad, Mark refused.

On Thursday night, Mark looked up the directions for 721 Sunset and wondered again what he had gotten himself into. When he awoke on Friday morning it was snowing. The ground had a light dusting, but not enough to get Mark out of the meeting. He grabbed a jacket and was out the door.

He arrived at the address at ten minutes before ten, thinking there must be some kind of mistake, seeing it was an abandoned lot. As he looked in his rear view, he saw Jim Clarke pull in behind him. Mark climbed out of his *Honda* and greeted Jim.

"Good morning, Mr. Clarke."

"Good morning, Mark. Why don't you just call me Jim?"

"Okay, Jim. But I must say, I am a bit confused about the address. What does a place like this have to do with my future?" Mark said with a strange look on his face.

"I thought you might be wondering that," Jim said with a laugh in his voice. He stepped between the cars and walked across the sidewalk onto the edge of the vacant lot. Mark followed.

Jim looked at Mark and said, "This place sure brings back good memories."

"Sir?" Mark questioned.

"This is where it all started, Mark."

"I don't understand sir."

"This is where I had my first job, Mark. I was nine years old and my mom had eight lemons sitting in a bowl on our kitchen counter. She liked the way they brought color to the kitchen, and so she often bought them, eight for a dollar, at the market over on Frazier Street. It is about a mile from here."

"You must have lived near here," Mark responded.

"I must have been driving my mom crazy for her to part with those lemons that day," Jim remembered.

He continued, "I took the lemons and started squeezing. We had one of those glass bowls with a knob sticking up through the middle for squeezing. You have probably never even seen one. Anyway, I squeezed up a pitcher of lemonade and like most kids, back in the day, I was in business. The first day I ended up with a dollar and twelve cents. I sold two cups of lemonade for a nickel a piece. My next door neighbor, Mr. Thomas, stopped by and gave me a dollar. Said it was for start up costs. And I found two pennies on the ground walking home. It was one of the best days of my life. That is, until my mom made me give her the dollar to pay for the lemons. But I was on my way."

How messed up am I to be standing in the snow listening to a man tell me stories about his childhood lemonade stand?

The words, "Let's take a walk, Mark," interrupted his thought.

Jim walked across the wet street and turned left on the sidewalk. About a block down, on the corner, was a small frame house that looked as if it might have three bedrooms at most. Walking up to the mailbox, Jim looked at Mark and said, "This is where I grew up, Mark."

Mark interrupted him, "Sir, I don't mean to sound rude, but what does all of this have to do with my future?"

"If only I had paid attention," Jim said with regret in his voice, as he stared at the house.

"Paid attention?" Mark asked.

"There were clues about me. Things I could have picked up on, only I didn't."

"What kind of clues, sir?"

"That summer I ended up making $183 selling lemonade on that lot back there. I discovered I had what it took to run a business. But my favorite part was not the profits."

"What was?"

"The people, Mark. I loved talking to all of the people. I should have realized people were more important to me than profits, but it took me a while to figure that one out. I will have to tell you more about that part later."

"I still don't see what all of this has to do with where I am going with my life," Mark said.

"Mark, I have found it is a lot easier for a person to know where he is going, if he understands where he has been. You need to look back before you look forward."

"This seems a little strange, if you don't mind my saying. I never had a lemonade stand or any other business for that matter. Not much to look back on, if you ask me," Mark said.

"That is where you are mistaken, Mark. Your life has been talking to you all along. There have been clues for you too."

Mark pondered this thought. "Clues?" he said.

"Clues, Mark. Everyone has them. And they are always present if you learn to pay attention," Jim said.

He continued, "Take Katie for instance. She didn't just grow into a love for numbers and finance, Mark. It has always been there. As a four year old she already had a grasp of percentages and statistics. It was weird compared to her friends at the park. While the other girls were playing on the swing sets and monkey bars, Katie was gathering pebbles and organizing them into groups of ten."

Mark laughed and commented, "I can believe that about her."

Jim laughed too. "When she was seven, she would memorize the stats on the back of her brother's baseball cards. She loved Math class. Every night she would ask me to give her some additional equations to solve. Her brother thought she was nuts. But it is who she is, Mark. It was true at eight and it will be true at eighty.

"Clues," Mark repeated.

"Clues, Mark. Which brings us to your homework assignment."

"Homework?"

"More like a project. I want you to identify three people who knew you before you were ten years old and give them a call. Ask each of them to identify three characteristics that were true of you when you were younger. Write down what they tell you and bring the list to our next meeting. And oh yeah, one of the three needs to be one of your parents."

"My parents! I am not so sure that is such a good idea," Mark responded with less than a pleasant tone.

"Your parents really do care about you, Mark. And they know what you were like when you were younger better than anyone else. It won't kill you."

Mark said, "I'll think about it."

"*Look back,* Mark. That is the place to start. Next month we will meet at *The Wake*. Bring your list."

With that, Jim Clarke turned and walked back toward the cars, leaving Mark standing on a sidewalk in the snow, once again feeling very alone.

The List

The next couple of weeks, Mark found it a bit easier to forget about his dilemma. Classes started and the campus came back to life.

Mark's class load for his final semester was manageable. He had two classes in his major, a required *Russian Lit* class he had been putting off for two years, and an elective in *Recreation: Camping, Rappelling,* and *Orienteering.* Compared to the past couple of years, the load would be a breeze. Three weeks after his "lemonade meeting" with Jim Clarke, Mark's smartphone beeped a reminder that his next meeting was only ten days away.

The weather, for January, was actually decent that day, so Mark grabbed a turkey and Swiss sub and found a sunny spot and sat down for lunch. He pulled out a pad and attempted to identify a possible list of people he could call who knew him as a kid.

Mark quickly came up with five names. By the time he had finished the sandwich, he had narrowed the list down to two. His fourth grade teacher, Mrs. Bush, and his Uncle Chuck.

Mrs. Bush, still to this day, was his favorite teacher. She

was like family to his mom, after several years of the two of
them walking together a couple of evenings a week. Mark
first met her during the summer after third grade. His dad had
just been promoted, which necessitated a big move for the
family.

Mark's mom, Anne, drove Mark to his new school during
late July, where they met Mrs. Bush, working on her room,
preparing for the upcoming year. Mark and his mom spent
nearly an hour talking with Mrs. Bush, and Mark even helped
arrange the desks while the two women chatted. Anne Johnson began a friendship that day that had only grown through
the years.

As for his Uncle Chuck, perhaps no one knew Mark better
than Anne's brother, Chuck. As a kid, Mark did everything
with his Uncle Chuck, who was married, but did not have
any children. He treated Mark like his own kid when the
two of them were together, which was often. Chuck took
Mark to ball games, rock concerts, on fishing trips, and even
taught him to swing a hammer. Uncle Chuck had a workshop that was second to none. It was Mark's favorite place
on earth. The shop had every tool you would ever need, was
perfectly organized, and was spotless.

As he ended his lunch, Mark made the decision to go
through with this crazy "assignment," as Jim had called it. He
would contact Mrs. Bush and his Uncle Chuck and see if they
could give him some insight into his past. Mark's mom would
round out the list.

Cartoons and Cathedrals

On Thursday afternoon at four, Mark made a call to his former elementary school and asked to speak with Mrs. Bush. He knew she would be sitting at her old brown desk grading papers as she had done for years.

Within a couple of minutes Mrs. Bush came to the phone in the school office. She was delighted to hear the voice of her former student.

"Hi, Mrs. Bush. This is Mark. How are you doing today?"

"Hi, Mark. I am doing great. How are you?"

"I am doing okay," Mark said.

"That's wonderful. Your mom and I were just talking about you last night on our walk," replied Mrs. Bush.

"Still walking with mom a couple of times a week, huh?" asked Mark.

"Trying to keep our New Year's resolutions," she said, jokingly. "What can I do for you, Mark? Is everything okay?"

"Everything is fine," replied Mark. "I actually need your help with a little project I am working on for school."

"I will help if I can," stated Mrs. Bush. "It has been a while since I was in college."

"Thanks. But it won't require your intellect. I need your memory. Actually, it is kind of silly. I am supposed to find a couple of people who knew me before I was ten and ask them what I was like as a kid. I thought you might be able to remember something."

"That sounds like an interesting class, Mark. I would be happy to give it a shot."

"Thanks," Mark said, rolling his eyes and wondering why in the world he was on the phone with his fourth grade teacher.

"Well. Let's see. First of all, you were a very good student. You worked hard, you were organized, had great handwriting, and you loved to draw."

"Draw?" questioned Mark.

"Don't you remember, Mark? You were notorious for illustrating your notebooks with cartoons and pictures," Mrs. Bush continued, "I also remember one certain project you did for our section on World History. You built a replica of a European cathedral that was the most elaborate thing I had ever seen from a fourth grader. Still to this day, I have not seen it's equal.

"I remember," Mark said. "My mom still keeps it in the storage room at the house; says it makes her want to visit Europe and see all of the cathedrals every time she looks at it."

"Well, if she decides to go, tell her I am in," said Mrs. Bush.

"I will, Mrs. Bush. Thanks for your time. You have been very helpful."

"You are welcome, Mark. Take care of yourself, and I hope the project turns out okay."

As Mark hung up the phone he looked down at his notes. He couldn't help but smile as he noticed he had sketched out a likeness of the cathedral during their phone call. It was time to call Uncle Chuck.

Uncle Chuck

"What's up, crazy man?" Mark said when he heard his Uncle Chuck answer the phone.

"Marko! Needing someone to bail you out of jail?" his Uncle Chuck joked.

"Not today," Mark replied. "Just calling to see how things are going."

"They are going fine here, but I heard you flipped out at Christmas. What was that about?"

"I don't know. Just feeling some pressure, I guess. You know— expectations from Dad and I just snapped. The whole thing was stupid and I probably didn't handle it very well."

"Nothing new," Chuck said sarcastically, lightening the mood.

"Listen, Uncle Chuck, I am working on this project and the assignment is to contact a couple of people who knew me as a kid and ask them what I was like. I thought you might be able to give me a couple of things you noticed about me."

"What kind of class is that, and what does your childhood have to do with Economics?" Chuck asked.

"It's not exactly a class. It's a long story." Mark paused. "Can you just give me something?"

"Yeah, sure. Well, let's see. You always seemed pretty

smart to me. You were great at concepts and how to build things when we were in my shop working. Whenever your mom let you come over to stay with us, you always brought your *Lego's* with you. I never could get you to go to bed. You always wanted to build things with those blocks, more than you wanted to sleep. You built a city one time that was nuts. I never knew where you came up with all of your ideas. I tried to help you, but I never could get those crazy things to un-snap."

"Anything else?" Mark asked.

"How about your art? Remember the way you could draw? You and I smoked your parents in *Pictionary* when you were only seven years old. I don't think we ever lost to them after that night. My guessing and your drawing were a lethal combo.

"Those were good times," Mark remembered aloud.

"Yeah, they were, kid," Chuck agreed.

The two of them talked for a few more minutes. Before they hung up, Chuck said, "Mark, call your old man and patch things up. He's not so bad."

Calling Home

Another week went by and it was Thursday evening. Mark's next meeting with Jim Clarke was scheduled for the following morning, and he still had not called home. About 9:00 p.m. he dialed his mom's cell. On the third ring, Mark was surprised when his father answered.

"Hello," came the voice of George Johnson.

Hi Dad. Is Mom available?" Mark asked.

"She stepped into the grocery store and I am sitting here in the car waiting on her to pick up a gallon of milk," George said, with a hint of impatience in his voice.

"Well, will you ask her to call me later? No big deal, just when she has time?"

"Yeah. Listen, Mark, you still thinking that nonsense about changing your major? You know, your little episode basically wrecked Christmas," George said with a sharp tone.

"It's not nonsense, Dad. Save the lecture."

"I am not trying to lecture you, Mark. It's just that people don't change their majors midway through their senior year. Think about how crazy that is, son."

"Believe me, Dad, I have thought about it. I think about it every day, and I have a future to consider."

"More like a future to throw away, Mark," George heatedly said just as Anne opened the door to the car.

"Is that Mark?" Anne mouthed as George finished his sentence. George nodded to her that it was.

"Make things right with him, George," Anne whispered as she raised her eyebrows and tightened her lips.

"I am not throwing anything away, Dad," Mark raised his voice back.

"Make things right, George," Anne whispered again,— only this time louder and with more force.

Mark sat there stunned. He was furious. Tired of the lofty expectations; sick of the same old scripted argument; and convinced he was done "looking back."

"Only my money!" George yelled, completely ignoring Anne. And with those words he hung up the phone and flipped it back into Anne's purse that was under her feet beside the console.

Mark sat there stunned. He was furious. Mostly, he was tired of the lofty expectations, sick of the same old scripted argument, and convinced he was done "looking back."

He needed to clear his head. He walked out onto the courtyard outside of his dorm. The night was clear and cold. The stars were brighter than Mark could ever remember. He decided to take a walk. Within minutes Mark was standing in the middle of the deserted academic quad. As he looked around at all of the buildings, his head began to spin with majors and career choices.

Maybe Dad is right? Maybe I am throwing away my future? Perhaps I should forget this whole mess and just finish my degree and get a job like we discussed?

But somewhere deep within, as Mark Johnson looked up at the sky, he knew there had to be more to his future than just getting a job and making a lot of money. His dad had gone that route and it had turned him into a jerk. Mark refused to go down the same path. Looking at all the different stars, Mark knew people were just as different. "I will find my way," Mark said out loud as he headed back to his room.

When he arrived, he gathered his notes from Mrs. Bush and Uncle Chuck. After the phone call to his mom that was ambushed by his dad, two out of three would have to do.

He pulled out a clean sheet of paper and a mechanical pencil and began to write.

Mark Johnson before age ten . . .
- Good student
- Hard Worker
- Organized
- Neat handwriting
- Liked to draw
- Good illustrator
- Made a replica of a cathedral

- Smart
- Great at building things
- Good at concepts
- Loved *Lego's* more than sleep
- Good at drawing
- Better than his parents at *Pictionary*

When he finished the list, Mark thought there might be a pattern, but he was not sure how to make sense of it all. *There are no jobs at playing Pictionary and Lego's,* he thought to himself. If there were, I would be set.

As he lay on his bed, for the first time, he thought Jim Clarke might be able to help him. He would hopefully find out in the morning.

The Finding Your Way Process

Step Two

LOOK IN

Frequencies

The first Friday in February found Mark walking through eight inches of new snow on his way to *The Wake* for his second meeting with Jim Clarke. A storm had blown through the area the night before and the world was a wonderland of white. *The street is so quiet and peaceful,* Mark thought to himself. He longed for a similar snow-covered-kind-of-quiet in his inner world but knew there would be none of that until he got his future sorted out.

As he walked in the front door, Mark patted his pocket reassuring himself that he had not forgotten his assignment. He was hoping maybe Jim Clarke would wave a magic wand over his *"Who I was Before I Turned Ten List"* and conger up what he should do with the rest of his life.

As Mark stepped in the front door, the coffee shop felt as quiet as the outside world. Only one student sat lost in her laptop at a corner table. *People must still be digging out after the storm,* Mark thought. As his eyes scanned the room he noticed Jim sitting by the fireplace in the same chair as their previous conversation. He was hesitant to disturb him because Jim looked deep in thought. The noise of the door closing caused Jim to look up. He waved him over and as the two shook hands he invited Mark to have a seat.

"It's beautiful out this morning," Jim said as they settled into their chairs.

"Sure is," Mark responded.

"The place should stay quiet for another hour because of the storm so let's jump into our next conversation," Jim suggested.

"Sounds good to me. I've got my *Look Back* homework here. Do you want to see it?" Mark asked.

"Not right now. Hold on to it because it will play a role as you do some directed thinking this next month," Jim instructed.

"And just what will I be thinking about?" Mark asked.

"Self-awareness," Jim said.

"Self-awareness?" Mark responded.

"Yep. It's one of your greatest allies when it comes to discerning the truth about yourself and your vocational direction."

"How so?" Mark inquired.

"Self-awareness is about *Looking In*, Mark. It is what allows you to notice when you come alive inside or when something puts you to sleep. It identifies when there is genuine interest or disinterest present. It helps you identify if you feel alive or bored at any given moment. It is an incredibly powerful weapon in the discovery process. If *Looking Back* is the first step in finding your way, *Looking In* is the second."

Intriguing, Mark thought. "Go on, I'm with you."

"You are twenty-one years old, right?" Jim asked.

"Right," Mark responded.

"Over the last two decades you have had hundreds of life experiences as a boy, a teenager, and leading right on into college. You've had part-time jobs, played sports, been on trips, met tons of diverse people, dated, gone to church, listened to music, been on vacations, traveled, had multiple classes with numerous professors, read books and so on. You've explored life in many different ways. You get the idea," Jim stated.

"I do. But what does self-awareness have to do with those?" Mark asked.

"As we live each day we bump into life. And as we do, we have inner reactions to the experiences we have. Learning to read from the pages of our life experiences is critical."

"The pages of my life, huh? I'm not sure I understand," Mark interrupted.

"Those who learn how to read their inner reactions begin to recognize what gives them life and what drains the life out of them," Jim revealed.

"You mean like Professor Horner's *Econ 301* class? That class sucked the life out of me. I had to do everything in my power to stay awake," Mark replied.

"Interesting. That was Katie's favorite class and professor."

"You have to be kidding," Mark responded. "If it wasn't for *Red Bull* I would have failed that class."

They both laughed.

"Think about what was going on there, Mark. How could two equally bright young people like you and Katie have such different reactions to the same professor and class content?

I will tell you how . . . topics, causes, issues, and vocations all send out different frequencies; like radio stations. Some stations broadcast on 91.4, others on 104.7. If Professor Horner's *Economics 301* class broadcasts at 91.4 and your inner tuner is pre-set at 104.7, there is going to be a miss. It will just be static to you," Jim explained. "You still with me?"

"I think so," Mark responded. "I just thought Katie was kissing up to the prof when she asked questions. She was actually 'tuned in' when she asked those questions, huh?"

"Absolutely. She'd come home and go on and on at dinner about some theory that was discussed that day. I didn't find many of the theories interesting, but I'm very interested in my daughter so I listened," Jim confessed.

"I can understand that. I have sat with friends who go on and on about stuff that bores me to tears but I listen because they are friends," Mark admitted.

"Let me ask you a broader question about your life experiences outside *Econ 301*. Were you at all aware of the reactions you were having and what they might be telling you about you when *you* had them?" Jim asked.

"I don't think so. I mean, I knew when something was interesting or boring to me at the time, but I didn't put together that those reactions had anything to do with what I should do with my life," Mark admitted.

"They did. Each of those reactions ignited a ticker-tape of data flowing from inside you giving an ever clearer picture of who you really are," Jim stated.

"That's pretty cool when you think about it," Mark

shared.

"It is more than cool. It can be life changing. Do you play the piano Mark?"

"Piano? Nope. A little French horn when I was in middle school. Why, will that help?" Mark mused.

"Reactions reveal, Mark. Don't forget that."

Smiling, Jim said, "Not really. But the piano offers a great illustration for understanding your real interests and the *Look In* step in finding your way."

"Lay it on me."

"A baby grand piano has eighty-eight keys with corresponding strings inside the body of the piano. I'm sure you've stood looking into one of these at some time in your life."

"I have. My gramma has a baby grand in her living room, so I know what you are referring to," Mark disclosed.

"Good. Do you know what would happen if you removed the top of the piano, leaned your head into the body of the piano getting down close to the stings and shouted loudly the word '*Hey!*'?"

"Gramma would yell at me and I wouldn't get dessert," Mark quipped.

Laughing, Jim said, "That's funny Mark. Seriously, do you know?"

"No idea. What would happen?" Mark inquired.

"The string that is tuned closest to the resonate frequency of the note you shouted would vibrate," Jim revealed.

"Really? That's cool, but I'm not sure I see the point. What does that have to do with my future vocation?"

"Everything," Jim stated. "I believe that you have strings inside of you tuned to certain frequencies. Your DNA, early childhood experiences, the values of your parents, and some would even dare to say, your Creator put them there."

"Okay. Interesting. Keep going."

"You said a minute ago that there are moments when you are incredibly bored and other moments when you feel awake or alive," Jim reminded him.

"That's right. No doubt about it. *Econ 301* was a snoozer. But the elective I took on *Art History*, I'm a little embarrassed to admit, I loved it. I didn't want the class to end. Is that weird?" Mark asked.

"Not at all," Jim responded. "I believe that when you feel alive inside, you are around a topic, cause, issue, interest, or vocation that's shouting *'Hey!'* and it's causing one of your strings to vibrate. That vibration will result in you feeling alive, interested, and energized. It awakens something that is deep and true inside you. There will be life felt when those strings are vibrating and if you can pay attention when this happens, you will be closer to knowing what you should do with your life," Jim instructed.

"Are you saying that when I was young and spent countless hours drawing and building with *Lego's* it might have been more than just childhood play? There may have been inner strings vibrating?"

"Maybe so, Mark. You would need a lot more life experience to confirm that, but I think you are starting to grasp what I am saying. You see, those reactions can be directional for you. Recognizing what repulses you, what calls to you, what you do that seems to make time stand still -- all those are critical to know. One of the most important self-awareness questions you can ask yourself is . . . *Where is the life for me?* If you can pay attention to when life is coming into you and when the energy inside you is rising, you will be on your way."

The thought of a person's vocation giving them life awakened a sense of hope in Mark. He knew his dad's life had been dominated for decades by obligation and not passion. The thought of his life playing out that way sickened him.

"I love the idea of doing work that gives me life. Is that even possible?" Mark asked.

"Yes. And paying attention to when you come alive inside is critical to *finding your way* to your vocational path. As Katie grew up, I watched when she came alive inside. When I noticed a glimmer of life in her, I would point it out and invite her to consider what her reaction was saying about who she was. Those were rich conversations that at times I felt were almost sacred." Jim paused. "Self-aware people pay attention to what is happening inside them as they move through life. *Why?* Because reactions reveal. Don't forget that, Mark; reactions reveal."

"I think I can see that now," Mark responded. "I have to admit this is new to me. I have never really thought of things this way."

"Few people do, Mark. Most just move through life and don't realize that the keys to who they are can be read from the pages of their life experiences and reactions."

"I'm with you, Jim. What next step should I take?"

"Good question because I'm ready to give you your second assignment. Go to the local art supply store in the next few days and buy a sketch pad or journal and a pen you like. Then find a quiet place and spend two hours thinking about your last four years at college. Make a list of what classes you enjoyed and the ones you didn't. Ponder which ones called to something *in you* and were easy to attend. Think about the part time jobs you have had and what you liked about each. Maybe you hated seventy percent of a job but enjoyed thirty percent. What were you doing during the thirty percent? Write it down. Think of any volunteer work you did and ask if, and why, it was meaningful. Ask why you made time for it. I want you to look for, and identify, those moments when your strings were vibrating. Does that make sense?" Jim asked.

"Yes. What do I do once I write those things down?" Mark asked.

"Once you have done that work, invite three or four of your closest friends out to dinner and share your findings. Tell them about the assignment and ask for their input and insights. After that meal give your mom a call and ask her for her thoughts on your reflections."

Jim noticed a hesitation in Mark and asked, "You okay with this?"

"Yeah, I'm just thinking it will be a little embarrassing to ask my friends about this stuff," Mark risked saying.

"You'll be surprised Mark. Your friends are trying to find their way too. This will generate some significant conversation. If you are concerned, invite Katie to the meal. She gets this stuff and will help keep the conversation on track." Jim suggested.

"Maybe I will. Thanks, Jim. I'm starting to feel a little hope," Mark confessed.

"We'll get there. Keep the faith, Mark."

"Where do we meet next month?" Mark asked.

"Glad you asked. Meet me at 432 Grove Street at 10 a.m. one month from today. You familiar with where Grove Street is?" Jim asked.

"Sure. What's there?" Mark asked.

"Now that's part of the fun. You'll see when we meet there. See you then," Jim responded.

Foot traffic in *The Wake* had picked up, so Jim excused himself to help behind the counter. Mark lingered for a couple minutes smiling as he thought about his gramma's reaction to him screaming into her piano.

Think Time

The next morning Mark was standing on aisle 3 in a *Hobby Lobby* debating between a *Zebra* mechanical pencil and a fat *Pilot Dr. Grip Gel* pen. He settled on the pen. He then wandered over to the row where the journals were found and picked out a simple lined *Moleskine* notebook that was black.

The rest of the morning Mark spent reading a chapter that had been assigned a couple of days before by his *Russian Lit* professor.

After lunch, Mark headed over to a nearby park to spend some time thinking about his life, just as Jim had suggested. He found a bench, opened up his backpack, and pulled out his supplies. *I feel like I'm a first grader on the first day of school,* Mark thought to himself. *I really need to get a life.*

As the doubt crept in, Mark wondered once again why he was sitting in a park on a sunny afternoon while his buddies were over at the sports complex playing a pick-up game of hoops. *I might be the lamest college senior in the country* went through his mind as he opened the notebook.

Mark soon had two columns neatly drawn on the very first page of the book. In one column he made a list of his favorite classes he had taken while in college. The list included *European History, Art Appreciation*, his current *Russian Lit* class, and an elective in *Landscape Design* he had taken with his freshman roommate, Kyle. Mark noted none of the classes had anything to do with his finance major. He also thought back to how much he had enjoyed his *Advanced Placement Euro* class in high school as well as Mr. Tyler's *Industrial Arts*. *IA* as they called it, was just a fancy way of saying shop class. Nevertheless, it had been Mark's favorite because during his junior year they had designed and built a small green house that was used to grow flowers. The flowers were made into arrangements by the school's *Home Ec* classes and taken to a nearby nursing home several times a year.

Next Mark made a list of classes he wished he could have dropped. Professor Horner's *Economics 301* topped the list. *Snooz-o marooz-o*, Mark thought to himself, wondering how it could possibly have been Katie's favorite class.

Mark came up with seven more on the *Most Hated Class List*, as he had titled it. Six of the seven were core classes within his major. *No wonder I am miserable,* came to mind as he stared at the page. The only exception was his sophomore *Political Science* class taught by a man referred to as Dr. Sahara because he was so dry.

As Mark looked over both columns he thought back to Jim's words, "Which one's called to something in you and which one's didn't?" He thought about the piano and the vibrating strings. Mark knew there was something to what Jim was saying, but he was still a bit confused. *There is still static on my station,* Mark thought, remembering Jim's words about the radio presets. He turned the page and began to draw.

Within minutes Mark had sketched out a sweet detailed drawing of the stone fountain on the other side of the park. The drawing looked impressive to Mark—a nearly perfect replica of the original. In light of the exercise, Mark could not help but admit he had a real talent for drawing.

Flipping the page again, Mark started two more columns. This time labeling them *Enjoyable Jobs* and *Hurry Up Friday Work.*

Mark's first observation was that he really did like to work. It made him feel good about himself when he recognized he was industrious. Lazy is overrated . . .

This part of the assignment was much harder. Mark had only had a couple of jobs in his life and it had been a while since he had been on a payroll. But he soon added a few volunteer things he had done, as well as the summer he helped his Uncle Chuck clean pools. Surprisingly, he was able to come up with a few thoughts.

Mark's first observation was that he really did like to work. It made him feel good about himself when he recognized he was industrious. *Lazy is overrated* passed through his mind. Mark also noted that his favorite things from past jobs usually involved building or designing things. Working on the greenhouse with Mr. Tyler made the list. So did building a deck and flower bed with Uncle Chuck around the Thompson's swimming pool. They had worked on the project for three weeks the summer Mark turned twelve.

Mark also noted how he had enjoyed mowing yards and working a few Saturdays as a referee for youth soccer in his hometown during his senior year of high school. He debated writing either in the notebook, knowing full well his future career was not going to be cutting grass or blowing a whistle, but he wrote both down anyway.

As Mark concluded the *Enjoyable Jobs* column he made five bullet points at the bottom.

- I like to work
- Time flies when I am building or designing
- I don't want to grow up and be a referee
- I love being outside
- Uncle Chuck was a terrible pool cleaner

The last bullet made him laugh to himself.

The *Hurry Up Friday* column was somewhat easier. It started and ended with the bank. Mark's dad, George, had made sure both of his boys had the opportunity to work summers at the bank where he, himself, was the Vice President at the time. The very first day Mark thought it was cool having a 'real' job, but that quickly changed. For two summers, Mark worked twenty hours a week doing data entry and preparing bank statements. The only thing that kept him sane was that he got to drive as a courier between branches on Thursday afternoons. The thought of being a banker made Mark feel sorry for his dad. Again, he made a list of bullets.

- I don't like paperwork
- I am allergic to dress codes
- Time screeches to a halt when I am staring at a computer screen

The list felt short and incomplete, but it was all he could come up with. As he closed the notebook, Mark thought sarcastically to himself, *I would definitely rather be a referee than work in a bank. I'm really narrowing it down.*

Pizza

The following day Mark ran into Katie coming out of the dining hall on campus. "What's up, Kate?" Mark asked, holding the door open for her.

"Hey Mark, how's it going?"

"Starving," Mark said. "I need food."

"It's not too bad today. I recommend the steak and lobster," Katie joked.

"Hey Katie. Speaking of food, I was talking to your dad the other day and he gave me another assignment concerning my future. He wants me to go out to dinner with a couple of people and run some stuff by them that I have been working on. He thought you might like to come along," Mark said awkwardly.

"So my dad is asking me out on a date with you?" came Katie's quick reply.

"It's not a date. It's just pizza. And there will be others there," Mark said, realizing his face was turning red.

"Oh, I see. And who are these other people?" Katie asked, with a smile on her face.

"I'm not sure," Mark said. "It is supposed to be some people who know me pretty well."

I'm a lunatic! Mark yelled at himself.

Katie let up on him and suggested, "Why don't you ask Justin? He knows you about as well as anyone. And I can ask Sara if you like. She knows you pretty well, as many times as we have all studied together."

"They may both think I am nuts," Mark replied, thinking to himself, *And they'd be right.*

"When did you have in mind?" Katie asked.

"How about Tuesday night? We can meet at *Toni's* at 8:00 p.m."

"Tuesday is no good. Sara has a class on Tuesdays. How about Thursday?"

"Thursday it is," Mark agreed.

As Katie walked down the stairs, she said over her shoulder, "Then it's a double date. I like those."

Mark rolled his eyes and could only laugh.

•   •   •   •

Later that afternoon, Mark decided to head over to the sports complex to see if he could find Justin. Justin was Mark's best friend on campus and could usually be found in a gym when he was not in one of his physical education classes. Justin had known since seventh grade he was born to be a coach after his playing days were over. Basketball was his first love. Unfortunately, he had blown out his Achilles tendon as a freshmen walk-on and never even put on a college uniform. After rehabbing the injury, Justin became the best intramural player on campus. As Justin's teammate for the past couple of years, Mark's job had simply been to get him the ball.

As expected, Justin was finishing off a pick-up game when Mark walked up. After he hit the last three shots, Justin simply walked off the court with his hand raised in triumph.

"There is nothing better than kicking around a bunch of fraternity boys," Justin said as he greeted Mark with a high five.

"Don't tell me you are still worried about finding a job after graduation? Finance majors all get hired and bring down the big bucks, Pal."

"You got that right," Mark agreed.

"Where you been the last couple of days?" Justin asked.

"Been doing some thinking," Mark said.

"Don't tell me you are still worried about finding a job after graduation? Finance majors all get hired and bring down the big bucks, Pal. I am the one who should be worried. Poor old school teacher is in my future," Justin said. "Hey maybe you can create for me one of those portfolios and help me manage my pension and recommend some cheap stocks? You know, buy low sell high kind of stuff," Justin quipped.

"Whatever," Mark popped back at him.

"Dude, you need to stop worrying. It is all going to work out," Justin said as they entered the locker room.

Mark said, "I hope so," and proceeded to tell Justin about meeting Katie and Sara for pizza on Thursday night.

Justin looked up and said, "Pizza? I'm in!"

• • • •

When Thursday rolled around, Mark and Sara were the first to arrive at *Toni's*. The place was jammed, but Sara had somehow managed a booth in the back corner. Mark joined her and within minutes, Justin and Katie both showed up.

"I'm starving," Justin said without even saying hello.

"You're always starving," the other three said in unison. After they ordered, it was Katie who initiated the conversation. "Guys, can you believe graduation is only a couple of months away? Seems like only yesterday that I was graduating from high school."

Ignoring her, Justin asked, "I wonder how long it will take them tonight. Last time they had my order out in seven minutes. I think the waitress was interested in me."

Sara rolled her eyes and said, "Please."

Katie continued, "Tonight is about more than pizza, guys. You may not know, but Mark has been meeting with my dad for the last couple of months. He's been helping Mark figure out his future. Mark is struggling with whether or not he wants to pursue a career in finance after graduation."

Mark sat there listening, secretly thankful that Katie had taken the lead. Justin interrupted his thoughts when he blurted out, "Rockefeller here is working on a portfolio for me."

Having been filled in by Katie before the meeting, Sara pursed her lips and gave Justin an evil stare. "Motor down, Meat Head," she said.

Mark suddenly had the feeling that this whole thing was a bad idea. He wanted to get up and leave. But as he had the thought, the pizza arrived.

For the next hour the four of them sat and ate while Katie guided an unbelievable conversation about how Mark was 'wired up.' Katie prefaced the time by saying, "Sara, you are one of the top finance students on campus. You love numbers and you are a meticulous, organized planner. So financial planning has been on your radar for the past two years. Whoever hires you is going to hit the jackpot."

This brought a smile to Sara's face.

Katie continued, "Justin, the same is true for you when it comes to coaching. Remember the conference championship game last year when I sat in front of you in the student section?"

Justin nodded, as he polished off his last piece of crust.

"Justin, you never second guessed Coach Howard, you were first guessing him. I will never forget how you knew exactly when he would call a time out and about who should be substituted and when. Then you predicted the exact play that won the game for us. It was weird if you think about it. Out of a couple of thousand students, you were the only one I heard saying that stuff. You are going to be an awesome coach."

As she made that last statement, Katie had Justin's full

attention.

Katie then said, "As for me, economics is my game. Someday I might explore politics, but only because the economy needs to be fixed and I would like to see if I could make a difference in the lives of people. The thought of that charges me up."

Justin thought to himself, *I would vote for you.*

Katie concluded her remarks by saying, "Now, Mark needs our help. We need to see if we can help him gain some clarity on his future." Looking at Mark, she said, "Mark, why don't you take it from here?"

Mark started by sharing his findings from his think time at the park. His bullet points served as a basis for getting them started. When he was finished, he looked back at Katie for help.

The three friends spent the next few minutes picking apart Mark's findings. The consensus was that Mark needed to lean into his ability to draw and design. Perhaps architecture? Maybe art school? Possibly even a home builder?

Mark left the restaurant with a newfound respect for Katie. He could see that her dad had really done a good job of helping her find her way. He also was certain that there was something to what was happening in him. He felt excited about the thought of pursuing one of the careers his friends had suggested.

It would not take long for the excitement to fade.

Talking to Mom

On the third ring, Anne answered the phone.

"Hi mom, it's Mark. How are things at home?"

Anne replied, "Hey Mark. Sweetie, can I talk to you in just a minute? I have my hands covered in flour from a pie I am baking for your dad. Here talk to him first."

Before Mark could say a word, Anne had handed George the phone.

"Hello," George answered in a hushed tone.

"Hi dad. How are things going for you?"

"Fine." George remained short with his son. "How's school?"

"It's okay."

"You still planning on graduating?"

"Yeah, dad, I am going to graduate with my finance degree," Mark said, wondering why the guy would never let up.

"I am glad to hear it. Well, here's your mother." George handed the phone back to Anne.

"Hey, Mark. Thanks for calling," his mom said with a smile in her voice.

For the next ten minutes Mark and his mom talked about the weather, his mom's plan for some upcoming spring cleaning, and about the woes of George being a bank president as he was having to let go of a couple of long-time tellers at the bank because of some downsizing.

The comment about his dad's job turned Mark's thoughts back to his own ordeal. He proceeded to tell his mom about the *Look In* exercise and about his dinner with his friends. Mark then decided to take a risk.

"Mom, I have been giving some thought to graduate school."

"That's great, Mark. Your father always says an MBA will only enhance your chance of landing a great job."

"I'm not thinking MBA anymore, Mom," Mark said, grimacing as the words came out of his mouth. "I am actually considering an architecture program."

"Architecture?" Anne questioned. "Wouldn't you need an undergrad degree in architecture to pursue graduate school?"

"I'm looking into it is all," Mark said backing off the subject. "Listen mom, I'd better go. I'll call you back next week. And in the mean time, would you mind not mentioning the architecture thing to dad? It's probably just a crazy idea."

As only a mother could, Anne affirmed Mark as they finished their call. "You will figure it all out son. I know you are going to do great at whatever you do. You always have."

Mark smiled as he hung up the phone, thinking to himself, *It is nice to have one sane parent.*

• • • •

With the noise of a basketball game on TV playing in the background, George Johnson sat in his comfortable chair lost in thought. He knew he had been short with Mark. He could feel his son slipping away; more accurately, being pushed away.

George knew in his heart Mark was a good kid: bright, creative, and hard working. *Why shouldn't he be passionate about his future?* The question raced through his mind and brought a wave of despair over him, knowing that the one thing missing from his own work at the bank was passion. George had plenty of money, a home without a mortgage, and was set to pick up a brand new car from the dealership in a couple of days. And yet, he sat there in front of his big screen television, experiencing a misery no one noticed.

Why shouldn't he be passionate about his future? The question raced through his mind and brought a wave of despair over him, knowing that the one thing missing from his own work at the bank was passion.

George's despair was interrupted by Anne's voice.

"George, why are you still being so hard on Mark?"

"I am not being hard on him. The boy needs to understand how the real world works," George retorted. "Life is not about sleeping in and intramural soccer. Neither of those will pay the bills."

Anne stood glaring at George without saying a word. The look said it all.

"What do you want from me, Anne? I have given that boy every opportunity under the sun."

"I want you to listen, George, and not react. Really listen to Mark," she answered. "He is a great kid with some incredible talents. He wants and needs your approval, but it seems you would rather be right than help Mark find what is right for him. This isn't about you, George. Don't forget that."

As Anne turned and left the room, George thought, *If only she knew just how much this is about me.* He felt lost as a dad and as a banker.

The Finding Your Way Process

Step Three

LOOK UP

Rev

432 Grove Street....Why does that address sound so famil-iar? Mark wondered as he drove to meet Jim Clarke for his third *finding your way* mentoring session. Turning onto Grove Street it hit him as he noticed the beautiful chapel that housed College Community Church.

Throughout his college years, Mark loved to wander around town admiring the architecture of old buildings and houses constructed close to a century ago. More than once he had stopped to take in the beauty of the neo-Gothic architec-ture of the Chapel. It was an impressive structure, and look-ing at it simply lifted his spirits.

He parked his car on the street in front of the Chapel and hustled up the front steps. Pushing through the large wooden front door he noticed Jim talking with a tall lean man. They were standing in the center aisle of the Chapel. Both greeted Mark with a warm smile.

"Good to see you, Mark," Jim said.

"Sorry I'm late," Mark responded.

"That's okay, it gave me a few minutes to catch up with a good friend. Mark, meet Reverend Moncree."

"Just call me *Rev*," insisted Reverend Moncree.

"Rev is a marathon runner, lover of great coffee, and the

senior pastor of College Community Church," Jim added.

"We've become pretty good friends since he moved to town three years ago to lead this church. Soon after arriving, Rev started coming into *The Wake* to drink coffee and work on his sermons. Every now and then, he'll ask for my opinion on an upcoming message. Rev likes to get some honest feedback before he delivers sermons and he's learned I always have an opinion on things," Jim revealed.

"Wonderful to meet you, Rev. This is one beautiful church you have here."

"Thanks Mark. You an admirer of architecture?" Rev asked as he noticed Mark surveying the wonder of the place.

"I am. Not sure exactly why. My eyes are just drawn to beautiful places like this and I always wonder what it took to plan and build something this spectacular. Besides that, when I was younger I made a replica of a European cathedral for a school project. It was also neo-Gothic, and I remember my mom reading to me about the large stone piers, pointed arches, and flying buttresses. Amazing stuff. And now, here those design elements are right before my eyes. Kind of takes my breath away," Mark confessed.

The three men stood quietly for a moment admiring the beautiful rainbow of colored light flooding through the stained glass windows that stood behind a suspended cross at the front of the Chapel.

"Jim tells me you are a senior at the college trying to sort out your future and questioning your current major. I'm guessing that's a frustrating place for you to be?"

"No doubt, Rev. It's really driving a wedge between my dad and me right now."

"I can imagine. I'm sorry that relationship is strained," Rev said as they all began to walk to the front of the Chapel. "How about if we sit down here on the front pew?" Rev suggested. "I'm still sore from a long run I took this morning."

As the three men sat down, Mark's eyes panned upward from the altar to the cross to the luminescent stained glass windows. *Man, this place is amazing. What would it be like to have been part of the group of artisans who built this?* Mark imagined.

"Earth to Mark. Earth to Mark," Jim said trying to bring Mark back to the conversation at hand.

"Sorry Jim, I was a little distracted. But I mean, come on . . . look at this place. Unbelievable. Simply, unbelievable. Okay, I'm back now." Mark responded with a smile.

"Mark, you've been at this *finding your way* process for a couple of months now. You have *looked back* by doing the *'Who I was before I was ten'* assignment. That exercise gave you some glimmers of who you are at your core. Next, we added another layer of understanding as you worked hard to listen to what your life may have been saying to you over the last four years as you assessed your inner reactions to your classes and experiences. You've certainly heightened your self-awareness. I'm proud of you for that. Today, we need to discuss the third step in this process. I've asked Rev to help with the *Look Up* step. *Look Up* has to do with recognizing both the spiritual nature of life, how sacred it is, and the responsibility we each have as human beings sharing this planet. This is the stuff a man of the cloth thinks about all the time."

Jim turned to Rev and said, "It's all you Rev. You can take it from here."

Mark wasn't sure why he felt a tinge of nervousness as Rev turned to address him. Maybe it was because he was not a regular church attender. He wasn't sure. He wondered if Rev was going to read the Bible to him or shout out a sermon or something. That is why it surprised him when Rev asked, "Mark, do you know if your dad was present when you were born?"

"I do," Mark responded. "He was there. He actually coached my mom through the entire birthing process for both me and my brother. They did the Lamaze classes and the whole deal. *Ah he, ah who, ah ha.* You know, the whole breathing routine. I've heard my birth story many, many times. Every year at my birthday party my dad would dramatically tell us kids how mom was in labor for seventeen hours before I popped out. He'd emphasize how worried he was that I'd never show. He even told the doctor that he had a tee time the next day at 9 a.m. and that if he wanted to get paid he'd better hurry this thing along."

"My dad would go on to explain how exhausting the birthing process was for him. Mom would always jump in and remind him that it was no picnic for her either. Dad was famous for saying, 'The day you were born was one of the most exhausting and exhilarating days of my life.'" Mark could not help but smile as he told Rev and Jim the story.

Mark glanced at Rev and said, "Boy, I haven't thought about this for a long time . . . but at the end of telling my birth story my dad would get all emotional. It wasn't unusual for him to tear up as he described what he felt the moment the doctor placed me in his arms. Then dad would go quiet and find it difficult to speak. When he caught his breath, he would say the meaning of that moment was just on the other side of words. We'd all sit still for a moment and then start kidding dad for being a softie and acting like a girl. He'd usually grab me, unleash an intense tickle attack and say, 'Yep, that was a great day, pal.'"

Mark paused. He found himself being moved by the telling of his own story, ambushed by the emotion that was squeezing his throat.

"Wow, sorry about that," Mark shared. "I haven't reflected on those birthday memories for a long time."

Rev put his hand on Mark's shoulder and said, "That's an awesome story, Mark. What a great memory. I'm so glad you shared it with us. Those were incredibly significant moments for your mom and dad. I know I cried when each of my three kids was born. What about you Jim?"

"Like a baby," Jim confessed. "Today I only weep that hard when Katie shows me her monthly credit card statement."

They all laughed and that felt good. It allowed Mark time to catch his breath.

Rev continued, "I think every parent feels the same way

when they look into the face of their newborn child. Each is struck with how sacred the moment is. It's almost holy because a miracle just occurred. A new human life has begun."

"King David wrote a beautiful prayer in Psalm 139. It's from the Old Testament of the Bible. In a moment of gratitude and clarity he thanked God for how he was made and who he was created to be."

> 13 *You made all the delicate, inner parts of my body*
> *and knit me together in my mother's womb.*
> 14 *Thank you for making me so wonderfully complex!*
> *Your workmanship is marvelous—and how well I*
> *know it.*
> 15 *You watched me as I was being formed in utter*
> *seclusion, as I was woven together in the dark of*
> *the womb.*
> 16 *You saw me before I was born. Every day of my life*
> *was recorded in your book. Every moment was laid*
> *out before a single day had passed.*
> 17 *How precious are your thoughts about me, O God!*
> *They are innumerable!*
> 18 *I can't even count them; they outnumber the grains*
> *of sand! And when I wake up in the morning,*
> *you are still with me!*
>   *Psalm 139:13-18 (New Living Translation)*

"King David knew his life was a gift from his Maker. He knew God had invested talents, gifts and passions in him and he found himself grateful for those. He lived his life with wonder and appreciation. This awareness birthed a sense of responsibility in him. Every life is amazing, including yours Mark. *Looking Up* understands this truth," Rev commented.

He continued, "You know Mark, when each of my kids was born I held them in my arms and wondered: *who are you, why are you here, and how do I help you find your place in this world?* I felt like something had just occurred that was so much bigger than me - something sacred. A new human life is awesome. It's a gift from our Creator and each child is incredibly full of potential."

"Have you ever been present at a live birth, Mark?" Rev asked.

"Nope. The only baby I've seen recently is my cousin's newborn and all I remember of that visit was that the kid could poop like an elephant and clear a room with the stink." They all roared at the thought.

"The Look Up aspect of finding your way is about respecting your life and understanding both the value and responsibility you have. It's foundational for responsible living."

Jim jumped back in the conversation, "When one has a quiet and clear head it's hard not to fall silent and *Look Up* acknowledging the gift of a new life, including yours, Mark. Then life happens and we lose the sense of wonder. Pressure, responsibilities, and the pace rob us of this awareness."

"The *Look Up* aspect of *finding your way* is about respecting your life and understanding both the value and responsibility you have. It's foundational for responsible living. It is recognizing that you are part of a much bigger story than just your own life. Your story is connected to generations past, present, and future. *Looking Up* acknowledges you have been blessed with a sacred trust of gifts, talents, and passions that must be identified, developed, and stewarded. It means you have a responsibility to this world to show up everyday in your own skin and contribute. Beginning each day, *Looking Up* frames your attitude as you bump into people and serve the world. The world needs the best and truest *you*. To me there is something very spiritual about that thought. This reality acknowledges your life has meaning."

Mark sat reflecting on the weight of both Rev's and Jim's words. Their comments did not feel like a sermon, they felt like truth. It was dawning on him that most of the world lives at the pace of modern culture and forgets the simple truth Rev just shared. Something rang true and deep about the Rev's words. They called to a place in Mark that few touch and he was realizing that was the type of life he wanted to live - grateful, responsible, and purposeful.

Mark turned to Jim and asked, "Okay, I hear you guys. What's the next step in applying the *Look Up* aspect of this process?"

"You're heading south this weekend for a week in the sun during spring break. Right?" Jim asked.

"As a matter of fact, I'm going to drive home Friday, do

some wash, say 'Hi' to my mom, and then meet some friends for the drive south on Saturday," Mark responded.

"Beginning each day Looking Up frames your attitude as you bump into people and serve the world. The world needs the best and truest you."

"Perfect. This next assignment is going to be tough for you, Mark. It will take more courage than any of the other work you have done thus far," Jim said with a serious tone.

"What is it? Do I have to drive the speed limit all the way to Florida or something?" Mark said smiling.

"Nope. But that's not a bad idea, Mr. Lead Foot. The assignment is for you to visit your dad when you get home on Friday and ask him to share your birth story with you once again."

"You're serious, aren't you?" Mark asked.

"As a heart attack," Jim responded.

The man will barely talk to me right now, Mark thought.

"I told you this one will call for some courage. I know you can do this, Mark. I can't wait to hear how this goes."

And with that Jim got up, excused himself, and headed back to *The Wake*. Rev said goodbye and hustled off to a counseling meeting with a couple who was struggling to keep their marriage together. Mark did not have to be anywhere, so he hung around for a few extra minutes basking in the beauty of the place.

As he looked up at the Chapel ceiling he chewed on what Rev and Jim shared about how sacred life is and the responsibility he had to fully bring himself to his work. Then he tried to remember the last time his dad shared his birth story. *I must have been twelve.*

After sitting for a half hour, he decided it was time to head back and get his final paper done before spring break. As he walked out the door of the Chapel he began plotting how he would approach his dad on Friday. *Why in the world did I ever step foot in The Wake?* he thought as the big wooden door shut behind him.

First National Bank

At 1:30 p.m. on Friday afternoon Mark stood at the front door of his dad's bank trying to rally the courage to enter. He paused to read the large cursive letters on the front door.

First National Bank
George Johnson - President

Mark's dad had worked hard over the years to reach the success he had earned in the banking industry. He had been President of First National for the last seven years and people respected both his integrity and work ethic. Mark also admired those things in his dad but wondered how in the world he could convince him that a vocation in finance was not right for him.

What was I thinking when I agreed to have this conversation? Mark thought as he pushed open the door. *I have to be out of my mind. My dad is not going to want to talk about my birth story. He's going to want to talk about an MBA and a future in finance that I don't want. Jim Clarke wasn't kidding when he said this would take courage.*

Mrs. Patty Porter had been his dad's administrative assistant since Mark was a boy. When she saw Mark coming in the front door she stood up and met him half way giving him a big hug.

"How are you Mark? I haven't seen you for a year. You look great. Are you excited about your upcoming graduation? Your dad is. It's all he's been talking about recently. He's so proud of you. And to think, you are following in his footsteps. Makes me smile every time I think about it," she effused.

'Same footsteps?' . . . If she only knew.

He thanked Patty for her kind words and inquired, "How does dad's schedule look this afternoon? Any chance of getting a few minutes with him?"

"I think his schedule is pretty open, Mark. I know he will be thrilled to see you," assured Patty.

Secretly, Mark had hoped his dad's calendar would be jammed so he could postpone this conversation.

"Grab a seat for a minute and I'll let your dad know you are here."

As Mark sank into the leather chair outside his dad's office, he wondered if his dad was still proud of him. He wondered if his dad would listen and understand his latest thoughts on his future or would have any interest in retelling his birth story. He also wondered if there was a back door to the bank he could sneak out of before his dad found out he was there.

Patty emerged from his dad's office with the news that George had one call to make and then he would be free to talk.

Five minutes later George Johnson invited his son to join him in his office. George shut the door as Mark entered.

"It's good to see you, Son. It's been a while since you've been here to the bank," George said as he sat down in one of the chairs in front of his desk.

"It has been, Dad. Patty is still as cheerful as ever."

"Best hire I've ever made. The woman is worth her weight in gold. I'm lucky to have her on the team," George quipped.

"What brings you by today, Son? Mom said you are heading to Florida for spring break. Do you need some money or something?" George asked without the usual edge in his voice.

"No. I'm good cash-wise, Dad. I didn't come by for that. I came by to talk about my latest thinking concerning my future and to ask a favor."

"Really? I'm glad you did. I've been doing some thinking about your future, too. You want to tell me your thoughts first or do you want me to go first?" George inquired.

"I think I'd like to go first if that's okay with you."

Settling into his chair George leaned forward and said, "The floor is yours, Son, I'm all ears."

Mark noticed that his dad was in a positive frame of mind and seemed sincerely glad to see him. He lacked the combative edge that had been present since their Christmas talk. Maybe it was because it was Friday and it had been a good week. Maybe he was relaxed because he had a light afternoon leading into the weekend. Or maybe Mom had softened him up a little through their conversations. Mark did not know, but he was glad for it, so he jumped into saying what he both needed and wanted to say.

"Dad, the first thing I want to say is that I'm sorry for the frustration I've caused you since Christmas. I shouldn't have just dumped my confusion on you on Christmas Eve. That was a bad move on my part. I am sorry about that," Mark confessed.

George watched Mark closely as his son shared his heart and found himself softening and being drawn to him as he spoke.

"And, as I've thought about my life and future over the last couple of months, some things have become clear to me. One is that I truly believe you love me and that you want me to succeed in life. That has been true since I was a boy, and I believe it's still true. I lost sight of that for a while. So, I'm sorry if you sensed an ungrateful attitude from me. Big picture . . . you have always been there for me and I want to thank you for that," Mark explained.

George watched Mark closely as his son shared his heart and found himself softening and being drawn to him as he spoke.

"Thanks for saying that, Mark. Apology accepted. We

haven't been on the same page for a while. I know I jumped to some conclusions on Christmas Eve rather than just listening. I reacted and didn't try to understand what you were feeling. Your mom tells me I do that now and then. Actually, she says I do that all the time," George admitted.

He went on to say, "It's been a long time since I was twenty-one and felt the pressures of looking at my future. Besides, I didn't have the choices people your age have today. Back then there was only one reality that drove vocational decisions . . . security. So, I chose finance for that reason. The truth is, I am not overly in love with this field, but it has provided a good life for us and it has paid for your education."

"I know, Dad. I appreciate it. I admire your success and respect how hard you have worked over the years. I also want to assure you that I am going to finish my degree in finance and graduate this spring."

"That's great to hear, Son. I think that's smart no matter where the future takes you," George stated.

"So can we start fresh today, Dad?" Mark asked.
"Deal," George replied.

George stood up, stepped towards Mark and gave the kid a hug that communicated they were once again on the same team. Mark felt a fresh sense of hope as his friendship with his dad was restored. Now he had to make his request.

"Dad, can I ask you for a favor that may sound a bit silly?" Mark asked.

"Do you want to take my new *Lexus* to Florida?" George responded with a smile.

"No, no, that's not it," Mark said.

"Then what's the favor?" George probed.

"Do you remember as I was growing up, every year on my birthday you would tell me the story of my birth?"

George smiled and said, "Sure do. It's a great story and I tell it very well, thank you. I also remember that when you reached ten years of age you would make fun of me when I would get emotional at the end and call me a sissy. I would have to put the 'tickle down' on you to get you to back off."

"I remember that too, Dad. Those are good memories. Would you replay that story one more time?"

"Glad to," he responded. And off went George Johnson with his tale of the birth of his son. He and Mark laughed out loud about the seventeen hours of labor, the *ah he ah who ah ha* feeble coaching of mom during the process, and the threat not to pay the doctor if Mark wasn't born before his tee time the next morning. Both men had tears in their eyes as George replayed the emotion he felt the moment Mark was placed in his arms.

When George was done with the story, they both sat silent together. There was no anger. No frustration. No judging. No controlling. Just a sense of wonder and appreciation for the gift of life and how good it was to be family.

"Thanks, Dad, for sharing that. I needed to hear it again," Mark admitted as he wiped his eyes.

"It felt good to tell it. I think replaying the story of your birth helps both of us have some perspective that will help us as we discuss your future," George exposed.

"No doubt, Dad."

"What do you say we get out of here and get something to eat? I skipped lunch today and I am starving. I really want to hear your latest post graduation thoughts, and we can do it over a sub or something. It will give us a chance to brainstorm options," George suggested.

"Perfect," Mark responded. "Let's go."

George told Patty he was calling it a day and, as they headed towards the front door, George tossed Mark the keys to his new *Lexus*. "Give me the keys to your car kid. You've gotta drive my new vehicle. It's a fantastic ride. I'll meet you at the sub shop on 40th Street."

Mark flipped his keys to his dad and for the first time in months he knew he was going to find his way into his future and that felt great.

The Finding Your Way Process

Step Four

LOOK OUT

Regents

It was 7:30 a.m. on Monday morning when Mark pulled into the *Regents Credit Union* parking lot. There were only four cars, including his, in the lot. On one of the cars he noticed Jim Clarke's custom license plate . . . *Wake Up.* The car was empty, so Mark assumed Mr. Clarke must already be inside.

Looking at the five-story building, Mark wondered why Jim would choose a credit union for their fourth meeting. He had learned by now not to question the man. Jim had not steered him wrong up to this point and after the breakthrough with his dad, Mark was eager to see how his immediate future would turn out.

Because of the early hour, the double glass door to the lobby was locked. No sooner had he pulled on it, a woman in her mid-forties stepped out from behind a reception desk and came over to unlock it.

"Good morning, you must be Mark. We have been expecting you. I am Lisa Thomas," she said.

"Good morning," Mark returned. "I am looking for a Mr. Clarke. He asked me to meet him here."

"Jim is making coffee in the break room. Down that hall, last door on your left."

Making coffee. It figures.

"Thank you, Lisa."

As Mark approached the entrance to the break room he was surprised to see a framed 8 x 10 photo of Mr. Clarke hanging beside the door. Below the frame was a placard that read, *Wake Up Like Jim.*

Bizarre, went through Mark's mind at the exact moment Jim called to him.

"Mark! Good morning. Come on in. I want you to meet a friend of mine, Daniel Williams. He is the founder and CEO of *Regents Credit Union.*"

"*One* of the founders," Daniel corrected him. "Good morning, Mark. Great to meet you."

"Good to meet you too, Mr. Williams," Mark said extending his hand.

"Jim tells me you are about to graduate from the university with a degree in finance," Daniel said to Mark.

"Yes sir. The big day is right around the corner. I never thought it would get here, but I just might make it if I can survive one more round of finals."

"I'm sure you will do great," Daniel replied.

During the greeting, Jim had returned to the coffee maker and started to pour. "Cup of coffee, Mark?" he asked.

"No, thank you," Mark replied.

"I brought a bottle of caramel from *The Wake*. The good stuff," Jim said smiling.

"All right," Mark said. "Hit me with it."

"Coming right up, kid. Eighty percent caramel and twenty

percent coffee."

"That's the way I like mine too," Daniel piped in.

"Why are we meeting here today, Jim?"

"Mark, there is one final piece to the *finding your way* puzzle that I felt I could explain better from here. Follow me," Jim answered, handing Mark his coffee.

With that, Jim Clarke walked through the door, down the hall, and to the elevator in the lobby. Mark and Daniel followed.

When they arrived on the fifth floor, Mark followed the two men to a large corner office that was set up like a living room. Comfortable chairs, a unique English pub table for writing, a small whiteboard on one wall and a portable fireplace with gas logs in the corner. In a peculiar way, the office reminded Mark of Mr. Clarke's back room at *The Wake* that Jim had shown him on the day of their first session.

"It's just like you left it, Jim. We kept it this way and decided to use it as a conference room," Daniel said as the three of them entered the room.

"Left it?" Mark said. "This used to be your office, Jim?"

Daniel answered for him. "That's right, Mark. Remember when I said downstairs that I was one of the founders of *Regents*. Mr. Coffee, here, was the other one. We were partners."

Mark stood there looking around the office in disbelief. Turning toward Jim, he questioned. "I don't understand."

"I'm afraid it's true, Mark. This was my former life."

"In truth, it was almost your former death," Daniel completed Jim's thought.

"Almost killed us both," Jim agreed, laughing.

"I'm confused, Jim."

"Mark, to be honest, this place was sucking the life out of me. The business was floundering. Profits were flat. All of us . . . Daniel, me, and the team were all frustrated."

"So Daniel let you go?" Mark said, still confused.

"No, Mark. I let myself go," Jim paused. "I stepped out. I quit. I chose to do something else."

"But if, back then, this place was so stalled, how did it get to be the best credit union in town?" Mark asked.

"One of the factors that helped move it ahead was that I decided to get out of the way so we both could succeed," Jim answered, with a touch of disappointment in his voice. "You see, Mark, who I am was not what the company needed at the front end."

"That is a bit of an overstatement," Daniel spoke up. "Jim was just not in his sweet spot, Mark. It was not that he couldn't do the work. The truth is, he is still the most relationally intelligent person this place has ever seen. The guy is a people magnet, as you well know. It was just that, in the early days, the work was not primarily people work. Most of the work revolved around setting up systems and structures. Those happen to be my strengths, not Jim's."

Jim picked up on Daniel's explanation. "It didn't take me long to recognize I had made a poor vocational choice given how I'm wired up. Building a big company was not my passion, so I decided to do what was best for *Regents* and sell

Daniel my half of the company. Turns out, *waking up* was what was best for me, too. I have never been happier or more successful in my life."

"Waking up, sir?"

"Yes, Mark, waking up. I was basically sleepwalking through my life, making a living, but not making a difference." Jim continued, "I guess you noticed my picture outside the break room?"

"I did. And the *Wake Up Like Jim* sign," Mark acknowledged.

"Yeah, well that picture is there because the break room was my favorite place in the building."

"Mr. Coffee," Daniel said, nodding to Jim.

"You liked hanging out in the break room and making coffee, Jim?" Mark asked.

"Not exactly. It was not that the intensity of the work made it necessary to take breaks all the time, Mark, or that I liked making coffee so much."

"The break room was where the people were," Mark interrupted, the light finally coming on in his mind.

"Exactly," Jim affirmed.

Daniel said, "But he did make a mean cup of coffee."

"I guess that makes sense all the way around," Mark said as if he had just discovered the secret of the man who was helping him find his own way.

"Which brings us back to your own puzzle, Mark," Jim stated as he motioned toward the meeting table. "Let's all have a seat."

The three of them each found a chair around the old oak table and made themselves comfortable.

"Mark, the fourth key to finding your way is to *Look Out.*"

"*Look Out*, Mr. Clarke? I'm not sure I follow you."

"It is not enough to *Look Back, Look In,* and *Look Up.* You must also *Look Out. Looking Out* is about the application of you in the real world. It's about aligning you with a specific vocation. It's collecting the insights you've gained about yourself over the last few months and assessing those against vocational opportunities," Jim commented.

"That sounds good. I've been kicking around vocational options in my mind. I was wondering when we were going to bring this all together. So how do I assess the possible options against who I am?" Mark inquired.

With that Jim stepped to the whiteboard. Across the top he wrote . . . *Mark's 'Finding Your Way' Matrix.*

"Mark, you should be drawing this. You are the artist among us," Jim observed.

"You are doing fine for a guy with a caffeine buzz," Mark said, cracking everyone up.

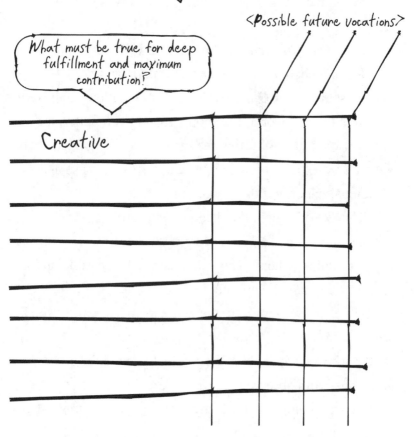

With one hand pointing at the freshly scribbled matrix and his eyes fixed on Mark, Jim added, "This matrix brings together the insights you have collected about yourself and allows you to assess them against vocational options. Down the left side in the horizontal spaces you record short statements that must be true of your next vocation if it is to fit you. These are the insights you've gained about yourself over the last few months. Then across the top you list vocational options. Does that make sense?" Jim asked.

"I think so," Mark responded. "Would the word 'creative' be one thing that must be true of my vocation if it is to be sustainable and fulfilling? Would I write that word in the left column?"

"Yes, I think so," Jim affirmed as he wrote it on the chart. "Take thirty minutes alone and fill this in as best you can. Write the personal discoveries you have made over the last few months down the left side and any vocational options you are kicking around across the top. When we come back Daniel has something he wants to discuss with you before you leave today. Sound good?" Jim inquired.

"Okay, I'll give it a shot. I'll see you guys in about half an hour."

As Jim and Daniel left the room Mark thought to himself, *Boy, I'm glad Jim is good with people because this drawing stinks.* Even Uncle Chuck could do better than this. He erased the white board, smiling, and drew a much cleaner, clearer, matrix and began to fill it in.

An Outrageous Opportunity

Jim and Daniel reentered the room with three fresh cups of coffee and a basket of snacks. Mark was admiring his work as he placed the top back on the whiteboard marker. They all paused and stared at the board.

Mark's 'FINDING YOUR WAY' Matrix

<Possible future vocations>

What must be true for deep fulfillment and maximum contribution?	Architect	Product designer	Landscaping	RCU expansion Intern
Creative				
Opportunity to design & draw				
Building something - Project managing				
Some work outside				
From concept to reality				
Challenging work				
Leverages art skills				

"Looks like you made some progress," Jim commented. "I see that you listed seven insights that are true about you—creative, opportunity to design and draw, building something-project managing, some work outside, from concept to reality, challenging work, and leverages art skills. Really nice work here, Mark. Seriously, each of these is true of you," Jim encouraged.

"You even wrote down three possible vocational paths across the top: Architect, Product Designer, and Landscaping. Beautiful. Although, I am a bit hurt that you erased my fine looking matrix and drew your own," Jim shared with a smile.

"Thanks for the encouragement, Jim. I did redo it. I didn't think you'd mind given that we'd all like to read it when it's done," Mark kidded.

"Not at all. It's just one more clue concerning who you are," responded Jim.

As they all reread what Mark had written one more time, Jim shared the final step in using the matrix to determine a future direction.

"Now the fun begins, Mark. For this chart to be useful you must grade each vocation against the statements on the left. In each small box you put a *'yes'* if the vocation will allow the statement to be true. For instance, would being an architect allow you to be creative? If the answer is yes. you write *'yes'* in the box," Jim explained. "On the other hand, if being an architect does not allow you to be creative you would write *'no'* in the box. If you aren't sure, simply place a *'question mark'* in the box. Got it?"

"Sure, that makes perfect sense. After assessing every vocation, I'm guessing that I step back and look for vocations that have the most 'yes' responses."

"You got it," Jim stated.

"This is starting to make sense to me. I can see how a vocation can flow from a person's passions and abilities. This *Finding Your Way* process rocks!" Mark blurted out as he sat down.

Jim and Daniel nodded in agreement.

As Mark settled into his chair, Daniel went to the white board and wrote a fourth vocational alternative at the top of the matrix. He wrote *RCU Expansion Intern*. With that he turned to Mark.

"Mark, I have something I would like for you to consider," Daniel began. "Jim and I have talked, and I would like to offer you a one year internship with *RCU*."

"You want me to come and work for your credit union? After all the conversation about living from passion and sustainability there is no way I can see myself in a finance field for the next forty years. Thanks, but no thanks. It wouldn't be right for either of us. That is one thing I am sure of."

"Hear me out, Mark," Daniel continued. "This would be a different kind of internship. Sure, I would like to tap into your financial training, but only in a limited way. Actually, I am more interested in your strengths as a designer and your ability to manage a project."

"I don't understand." Mark questioned. "What kind of project?"

"Mark, *Regents* is about to undertake an expansion over the next year. I just signed the papers with *King Construction* to build two new branches in the city over the next eighteen months. I have in mind the design that I want, but I think you could help me with some of the details and act as a liaison between an architect and *Regents*. You could also keep an eye on the construction, monitoring the budget and learning the business from an inside look. I couldn't pay you a lot from a salary standpoint, but I am willing to make a substantial financial investment."

Mark, hardly believing what he was hearing, remained silent.

Daniel continued, "The job would be for thirty hours a week, but there would be another twenty hours required for my other offer."

"What other offer?" Mark asked.

"I want to pay for you to go to school for at least another year," Daniel answered.

Jim picked up, "Mark, two years ago, the University began a program in *Architectural Design* with a minor in business."

"I'm familiar with the program. I even considered it going into my junior year, but my dad shot down the idea," Mark replied.

"Last week, I called Dean Riley, Mark. I mentioned your scenario to him and asked him if he had any recommendations on what you might be able to do. He said he needed to think about it. Yesterday morning he called me back and told me they are willing to petition the board on your behalf. He said with your finance major and with all of the business classes you have had, they are willing to design an MBA with a concentration in *Architecture*. You would need to take about forty additional hours to complete the degree. Over half of them would be in the architecture school, both undergrad and graduate. Along with the internship with Daniel, it would take you about two years to fulfill the requirements."

Daniel kept it going, "With a small salary, and I mean real small, you would be able to find room and board and I would be able to pay for your school, Mark. At the end of a year we could evaluate how things are going. If you are doing a good job for me and if pursuing the degree energizes you, I will agree to continue it for a second year. Then we would be at the opening date for our two new branches. If either of us feels it is not a good fit, we can part ways with no strings attached. Either way, you will gain some experience and earn at least a year of graduate school. It wouldn't cost your family a dime."

Mark sat there stunned. He asked, "What's in it for *Regents*?"

"Like I said, I need someone to help me manage this project— someone I can trust and who is motivated to do a great job. You could potentially save me tens of thousands of dollars over the next couple of years. Four semesters of graduate school is a small price to pay for that kind of return. Besides, I might be able to help you *wake up* like old Jim here."

Mark's mind raced with the possibility. He could feel the

adrenaline pumping through his veins. "So, when will we know for sure?" he asked.

"Dean Riley says they should know something in about a week. In the mean time, I think it would be good for you to think it over and ask yourself if this is really something you could see yourself doing," Jim said.

"That sounds good. I will," Mark said.

With that the meeting ended. Mark stood and shook hands with Daniel and thanked him for taking the time to meet with him and for the potential offer. Jim and Mark walked out together. *Regents* was now buzzing with activity as they exited the building.

Standing beside the cars, Mark turned to Jim. "Thanks, Jim. I really appreciate all you have done for me these last few months. Whether the internship works out or not, I have learned a whole new way of looking at my life from the time we have spent together."

"You are welcome, Mark. I will give you a call as soon as I hear from the dean."

With that, Jim climbed into his car and pulled out of the lot. As he drove away, Mark stared at Jim's license plate . . . *Wake Up*.

The Call

The following Saturday morning the University athletic department was hosting a one-day, end-of-the-year, two-on-two basketball tournament. Mark had bribed Justin to play with him by offering to buy pizza at the end of the day. The two had just finished putting a beat down on a couple of hot-shots when Mark's cell phone buzzed. It was the call he had been waiting for concerning Dean Riley's decision.

"What's up, Jim?" Mark answered.

"Hey, Mark. Have you got a moment?"

"Absolutely. I've been waiting for your call. This has been the longest week of my life. What did Dean Riley and the University board decide?" Mark asked as he grabbed a white towel and wiped the sweat off his face.

Jim could hardly wait to tell him, "It's a thumbs up, Marko. The University is willing to design an MBA with a concentration in *Architecture*. Can you believe it?"

Mark put his hand over his eyes as they filled with tears. It had been almost five months since the Christmas Eve blow up and the suffocating feelings of disillusionment he experienced on the long drive back to campus that night. Now, he had a future and a hope, one he could not have imagined a year ago. Mark struggled to say, "Unbelievable, Jim. From the bottom of my heart, thanks."

"My pleasure kid," Jim assured.

After taking a deep breath, Mark communicated to Jim that he was ninety-nine percent sure he was going to go for the *RCU Internship* and MBA program. It just felt to him like it was the right decision.

On the heels of that statement, Jim suggested they meet the following Friday for one final debrief. He asked Mark to compose a one-page summary of what he had learned through the *Finding Your Way* process they had walked through over the last four months. He told Mark to write his key discoveries on each of the four steps - *Look Back, Look In, Look Up* and *Look Out*. Mark agreed, and they decided the best place to meet would be *The Wake* at 10 a.m.

As Mark hit the *Off* button on his phone, the tournament officials alerted him and Justin that their next game would start in five minutes. Turning to Justin he said, "Feed me the rock, big boy. I'm on a roll today."

One Last Latte

It was eight days before graduation and *The Wake* was unusually crowded for a Friday morning. Jim suggested they sneak into his back office for their final meeting.

As Jim cleared books off a chair so Mark could have a place to sit he asked, "How'd the two-on-two tournament end up last Saturday?"

"Got to the finals, but I ran out of gas. Eight games back-to-back on one day did me in. Justin was a little upset with me for flaming out, but a pitcher full of *Coke* and an extra large *Meat Lovers Pizza* calmed the boy down," Mark reported.

"Katie tells me that kid is a piece of work," Jim chuckled.

"He's the best, Jim— silly at times, a huge eater, a bit too competitive, but a great friend," Mark assured.

As Jim settled into his chair, he paused and took a long look at Mark. To Mark, it felt as if Jim was looking right through him. Jim had the look of a professor at graduation as she looked at a prize student or a father at the wedding of his much loved son.

For Mark, it felt good to be seen. Jim had helped him look closely at himself and recover the truth of who he was created to be. *What a gift this is. One I certainly don't deserve, but gratefully receive.*

Jim broke the silence. "Okay, Mark, as we finish today I want to hear what you have learned over the last four months. Knowing that you are taking the *RCU Internship*, tell me how the four step process has helped you with that decision."

"I'll give it a shot, Jim."

"What I learned in the *Look Back* step is that there are clues to be discovered concerning who I am at my core by looking back at who I was before I turned ten. Taking time to investigate who I was back then felt a little silly, but when I got further into the process it made total sense. Talking to Mrs. Bush and Uncle Chuck helped me remember that I love challenging work, I am good at design, can create drawings and buildings from my imagination, and can illustrate with the best of them. My role at *RCU* will use all of those strengths."

"The *Look In* step might have been the most insightful for me. I learned through it that self-awareness is an incredibly powerful tool in the discovery process. It's my #1 ally when it comes to discerning the truth about myself and my ultimate vocational direction. I understand now that as I bump into life, I will have inner reactions to the experiences I encounter. Learning to read from the pages of my life experience is critical and a whole new way to look at things. Learning to answer the question - Where is the life for me? - identifies and exposes core truths about me. I'm paying attention to those. I have to tell you, Jim, as Daniel was explaining the internship at *RCU,* my heart was pounding out of my chest. I felt more excited, energized and challenged as I listened and even more so as I have thought about it now for a couple of weeks."

"The *Look Up* step affirms I was uniquely knit together before I was born by a power greater than myself. It reminds me that I need to daily see my life as a gift. It acknowledges that I'm part of something bigger than myself. It recognizes I have been blessed with a sacred trust of talents, abilities, and passions that must be identified, developed, and stewarded. When I look up I realize I was created for the kind of work I'll be able to do at *RCU*. It seems like the role aligns with who I am."

"Last, the *Look Out* step is about the application of me in the real world. I was able to take the collected insights gained about myself over the last few months and assess those against existing vocational opportunities. The matrix was awesome and I'll carry that construct with me for the rest of my life. There is no question that grading out the *RCU Internship* within the matrix revealed that it is a wonderful next step for me."

With that Mark concluded by asking Jim, "How'd I do?"

"Fabulous, Mark. Just fabulous. Congratulations, my young friend. You have indeed found your way, and I couldn't be more proud of you."

"There is something that I want you to remember, Mark. *Finding Your Way* is a process of discovery. Don't forget it's a process. The process is ongoing and as you lean into it, you learn more and more about yourself. As you do, act on that truth. Today you are acting upon what you currently understand to be the truth about you. If your findings are accurate, they will be confirmed over time and with additional experience. You arrived at where you are today by working this process. Make sense?" Jim asked.

"Absolutely," was Mark's response.

"I have one final assignment for you, Mark. Doing it well will allow you to finish the process strong. It will take the best of your thought to complete," Jim cautioned.

"Sounds serious," Mark quipped.

"The assignment is to write a letter to your dad explaining what you have learned since Christmas Eve. Share with him the *Finding Your Way* process and how it has helped you. Let him get a sense for the work you have done and tell him you are pursuing the *RCU Internship*. Put this in written form. It will take a morning of your life, but it will be well worth it. Any questions?" asked Jim.

"Nope. I'll write it tomorrow morning and get it in the mail to him so he gets it early next week."

"Perfect, Mark. It has been a joy meeting together. Don't be a stranger to *The Wake*. You know where to find me if you need me," Jim finished.

Mark thanked Jim again as they shook hands. As the two walked to the front door of *The Wake*, Mark paused to inhale the aroma of fresh coffee. Jim noticed and offered him a cup to go. Mark accepted, and as he walked out the door he took a sip, thinking to himself: *Who knew coffee could change a guy's life?*

Mark's Letter

As Patty Porter handed George the morning mail, the letter on the top of the stack caught his attention. George recognized the perfect script handwriting as being Mark's. He opened the envelope with an antique letter opener that Anne had given him when he was promoted to bank president. The letter inside was long and felt weighty. George began to read.

For the next fifteen minutes George read Mark's finding your way story. His emotions were a roller coaster . . .

For the next fifteen minutes George read Mark's *Finding Your Way* story. His emotions were a roller coaster as he thought back to Friday night *Pictionary* games and reflected on who Mark was before he was ten. George realized Mark had pegged himself as he read the *look in* section of the letter. He reminisced over Mark's birth story and actually felt tears streaming down his face as he reflected on their conversation the afternoon before spring break. Stopping by the bank had taken bravery on Mark's part. George could not deny that fact.

Mark outlined the internship at *RCU,* stating he was going to pursue the opportunity, but that he would feel better about it if he knew he had his dad's support.

As he finished the letter, George could not help feeling a measure of pride. It was obvious Mark had done some real work to gain clarity on his future. Doing so in the face of an unrealistic father who had failed to listen to him over the past couple of years had required courage.

George's pride quickly faded. He felt ashamed of himself. Looking around at the rich mahoganies of his corner office, George realized Mark was on the path to finding something that he, himself, was missing.

No one could deny that George was successful. He had an office full of plaques and accolades from various civic organizations to prove it. Through the years, he had granted loans to practically every major business in town—but success was not enough. Inside his chest he also longed to be significant. He was not even sure he knew what that meant for someone his age, but he knew he needed to find out before it was too late. Successful George Johnson was middle-aged and miserable.

Graduation

"You look so handsome, Mark," his mom doted. "Stand beside Katie and let me take a picture of the two of you."

Looking at Katie, Mark rolled his eyes as if to say, *Sorry my mom is acting like a tourist who just got her first camera.* Katie smiled and stood next to Mark posing for Mrs. Johnson.

The two families had met for breakfast at *The Wake* on the morning of graduation. George and Jim had hit it off quickly, commiserating together over how broke they were now that their respective nests were empty.

"Mark tells me you are the one who is most responsible for helping him sort out his future, and that you helped him land this internship. I really appreciate all you have done for him, Jim," George said warmly.

"I am not sure I can take any credit. Mark is the one who did all the work. He is a remarkable young man. You should be proud of him."

"I am proud," George agreed.

The afternoon was a blur for Mark as he posed for pictures with his Uncle Chuck, Mrs. Bush, who had driven up for the ceremony, and even Daniel Williams from *RCU* who was there to watch Katie walk across the stage.

"Stand there with your new boss, Mark," Anne said, as

she reached over to straighten Mark's tie and brush the lint off his graduation gown.

"That's a good idea, Sis," Chuck said, recognizing that Mark was embarrassed. Chuck couldn't resist adding, "You look good wearing that commencement dress standing with your new boss, kiddo."

Mark couldn't help but smile as Daniel leaned over and whispered to him, "Don't sweat it, Mark. I know how you feel. My mom was a scrap booker."

Epilogue

On the drive home the car was silent. George Johnson was once again wrapped up in his thoughts. While Anne sat in the passenger seat scrolling through the photos in her digital camera, George scrolled through his own set of images: Mark storming out the door on Christmas Eve; flipping the phone into Anne's purse at the grocery store; his wife's living room stare; a letter opener; mahogany walls; his name on the bank marquee; loan applications; countless civic gatherings; and the courage of his son.

A caldron of emotions washed over George as he thought back over all of the negatives of the past four months coupled with Mark's ultimate resolve. He could see the keys to the *Lexus* flying through the air to Mark after their office embrace.

There has to be more for me, too. My soul feels like it's shrinking. Something must change or I'm going to wither and die. This is more than just a phase. These were all thoughts that occupied George's mind with the passing miles.

Just like Mark on Christmas Eve, George hoped the timing was right as he opened his mouth and said, "Anne, we need to talk."

Coming in 2015

Join us on the continued journey of Mark's dad,
George Johnson, as he experiences breakthrough out
of his numbing mid-life struggle into a
life of clarity and meaning in
Dan & Randy's next book,

FINDING YOUR WAY TO RENEWAL

Next Steps

Finding Your Way is what all of us need. Past readers have shared that the story about Mark Johnson stirred a variety of thoughts and emotions. Some readers admitted the fable reminded them that their life really does matter and they need to live it -- today. Some confessed they needed a nudge (or even a swift kick) to reengage life fully and the story did that for them. Others have shared that the fable gave them the courage to reconsider whether or not they are living the life they are meant to live. Many younger readers mentioned that the process gave them a mental compass that will help guide them into their future. Most encouraging have been the comments of parents who have been inspired to better help their children find their way. What has been your reaction? What next steps do you need to take to *find your way*?

The most important thing to do first is to walk yourself through the *Finding Your Way* process. *Looking Back, Looking In, Looking Up* and *Looking Out* will only increase your sense of meaning, purpose, and clarity for your future. Personally going through the process is also a prerequisite if you want to help others find their way -- especially your kids. Here are two ways to engage the process.

The **first** way is to simply use the overview of the *Finding Your Way* process on the next few pages. Each of the four steps are outlined with suggested actionable *to do's* that will generate data that you can use to get a better picture of yourself. There is also a blank matrix ready for you to insert your personal findings.

The **second**, and most effective way to experience the process, is to work your way through the *Finding Your Way Journal* beginning on page 125. As you work through the journal you will be creating a permanent record of the insights you will collect as you read from the pages of your life story.

Below is a summary of the *Finding Your Way* process. Use this, and the Matrix that follows, to help you begin to gain clarity on your life and future.

Finding Your Way Process

LOOK BACK	THEME: *"Look back before you look forward."*
Focus	Look for clues that point to who you really are.
To Do #1	Identify three people who knew you before you were ten years old and call them. Ask each of them to identify three characteristics that were true of you when you were younger. (One of the three needs to be one of your parents if they are alive and able to be contacted.) Expect that the unseen will be revealed to you with time.
To Do #2	Make a list based on the conversations.
To Do #3	See if you can find photos of yourself before you were ten that reveal insights about who you are.
LOOK IN	THEME: *"Self-awareness is looking in."*
Focus	Learning to read from the pages of our life experiences. Reactions reveal. What are you reacting to?
To Do #1	Make a list of classes you have taken and which ones you enjoyed and which ones you did not.
To Do #2	Think about the jobs you had part time, full time. What did you like about - dislike about them? Note: were there jobs you had that overall you disliked but there was a portion of it you did like?
To Do #3	Think of any volunteer work you've done. Was any of it meaningful? Why?
To Do #4	Invite three or four of your closest friends out to dinner and share with them your findings. What are their responses?
To Do #5	Do you have anything you are passionate about? What?

Finding Your Way Process *continued*

LOOK UP	THEME: *"Recognize both the value of life and the responsibility we each have to contribute as human beings sharing this planet."*
Focus	You have a responsibility to use the gifts you were given.
To Do #1	If possible, ask one or both of your parents to share the story of your birth.
To Do #2	Spend some time clarifying the value of each human life within your personal faith or world view. Write a paragraph defining why human life is valuable and full of potential.
To Do #3	Identify two people who seem to live with a *Look Up* attitude. These people show up each day and use their talents for the good of the world. Ask them *why* they do this and *how* they rally the energy to pull it off.
LOOK OUT	THEME: *"The application of you in the real world."*
Focus	Aligning yourself with a specific vocation and finding your sweet spot.
To Do #1	Fill in the **Finding Your Way Matrix** [use the grid on the next page] • Down the left record the statements that are true about you. Use the information you gleaned from the exercises: *childhood interviews, reactions, classes liked and disliked, jobs liked and disliked, insights from friends.* • Across the top write vocational options that excite you. *Note: Can't think of many options? Find someone who has a diverse job background or a leader of a company and solicit their input.*
To Do #2	Inside the grid put a *'yes'* in each box if it would make the statement about you on the left true, *'no'* if it would not. Place a *question mark* if you aren't sure. Where are the most yeses? What do they mean?

Mark's Matrix

Across the top write vocational options that excite you.

Record statements below that are true about you that need to have expression in your vocation.

Inside the grid boxes above put a **"YES"** if the statement about you in the left column would be true in the vocation, **"NO"** if it would not be true, and a **"QUESTION MARK" (?)** if you aren't sure. Then consider - where are the most 'yeses' and what do they mean?

DISCOVERING THE TRUTH ABOUT YOU

JOURNAL

FYW Publishing LLC

Finding Your Way Journal
Copyright 2014 © by Dan Webster and Randy Gravitt

ORDERING INFORMATION
FYW Publishing LLC
550 Old Orchard Road
Holland, MI 49423
Tel: 616-335-8500
www.findingyourway.us

Library of Congress Cataloging-in-Publication Data

Webster, Dan & Gravitt, Randy.
   Finding Your Way Journal, discovering the truth about you

   ISBN 978-0-9858896-1-6
   1. Self-Leadership. 2. Self-Discovery. 3. Vocation.
   4. Goals (Psychology). 5. Spiritual Growth

Scripture quotation (Matthew 23 reference) is taken from the Holy Bible, New Living Translation, copyright ©1996, 2004, 2007 by Tyndale House Foundation. Used by permission of Tyndale House Publishers, Inc., Carol Stream, Illinois 60188. All rights reserved.

Second Edition

Design work by Troy Murphy.
Troy is a gifted creative solutionist.
troy@launch137.com.

Finding Your Way Journal

Hugo is an extraordinary movie directed by Martin Scorsese and written by John Logan. A central theme of the movie is the journey to discover one's way . . . one's purpose. Sound familiar? The central character of the movie is a 12-year-old-boy named Hugo. Hugo is an orphan who lived in the walls of a railway station in 1930s Paris.

How in the world did he find himself living alone in the walls of a train station? Hugo had a caring father who loved and taught him how to build and fix things mechanical. Following his father's tragic death, Hugo's alcoholic uncle, who was the keeper of the train station clocks, takes him in and teaches him the fine points of clock adjusting. Upon his uncle's disappearance and death, Hugo continues to live alone in the clock tower. Hugo learns to survive living alone by stealing food and avoiding the clock tower constable. In the middle of his difficult life he keeps the clocks running smoothly.

On one of his escapades, he meets George (Papa George) Melies, a shopkeeper, who works in the train station and his adventure-seeking god-daughter, Isabelle. Isabelle and Hugo become close friends. Soon, after trust is built in their friendship, Hugo invites Isabelle up into the clock tower to see how he lives.

In a powerful scene, Hugo and Isabelle are sitting in the clock tower observing the activity in the train station below. Hugo notices Monsieur Labisse. Monsieur Labisse is the owner of a bookstore. He is a generous man who loves to share his books with those who may need the lift or challenge that only a book can bring. Hugo notices Monsieur Labisse giving a book to one of his patrons. Moved by the man's generosity, Hugo turns to Isabelle and says . . .

Hugo: Monsieur Labisse gave me a book the other night.

Isabelle: *He's always doing that, sending books to a good home. That's what he calls it.*

Hugo: He's got real . . . purpose.

Isabelle: *What do you mean?*

Hugo: Everything has a purpose. Even machines. Clocks tell the time and trains take you places. They do what they are meant to do. Like Monsieur Labisse. Maybe that's why broken machines make me so sad. They can't do what they are meant to do. Maybe it's the same with people. If you lose your purpose, it's like you are broken.

Isabelle: *Like Papa Georges.*

Hugo: Maybe we can fix him.

Isabelle: *Is that your purpose? Fixing things?*

Hugo: I don't know. It's what my father did.

Isabelle: *I wonder what my purpose is?*

Hugo: I don't know.

Isabelle: *Maybe if I'd known my parents I would know.*

Hugo: Come with me.

Hugo invites Isabelle to a different location in the clock tower that overlooks Paris. They are standing looking at the city below through the clear glass face of a large clock when Hugo comments . . .

Hugo: Right after my father died, I'd come up here lots. I'd imagine the whole world was one big machine. Machines never come with any extra parts you know. They always come with the exact amount they need. So, I figure if the entire world was one big machine, I couldn't be an extra part. I had to be here for some reason. And that means you have to be here for some reason too.

Isabelle looks intently at Hugo as he speaks. When he finishes sharing his thoughts, she smiles, takes his hand and they stare quietly at the busy city below.

Hugo and Isabelle are not the only people attempting to find their way. They stood overlooking the city of Paris discussing some of life's most important questions. *Am I here for a reason? What is that reason? Does my life have a purpose? How do I find my purpose?* Today, wherever you live in this big world, you are focused on *Finding Your Way* . . . working to discover your purpose. For Hugo and Isabelle, it took time, energy and courage. But they discovered that they indeed were here for a purpose. If you faithfully work the *Finding Your Way Process* in these pages you will discover the same.

The Purpose of the Finding Your Way Journal

The *Finding Your Way Journal* is about **YOU** -
- your **purpose**,
- your **contribution**, and
- your **place in the world**.

The *Finding Your Way Journal (FYWJ)* will **help you discover or rediscover the truth about you**. The work you are going to do on these pages will help you clarify who you are so that you will have an increased confidence to live into *you* everyday. The ultimate goal is that you will live the life you are meant to live.

The *FYWJ* will **provide you with a process of discovery.** The work this journal will lead you through offers a way to help you gain perspective on yourself. You will hike up the mountain of your life experience, turn around and look over the valley floor of your life. In the end you will see yourself more clearly. You will have a much better idea of what interests you, what gives you energy, and how your life should touch the world around you. This knowledge can help guide you to make far better decisions when it comes to choosing a major in college or your next vocation. It will literally cut through the fog that clouds your future.

Let's say it again . . . the *FYWJ* is **a process**. Hold onto that truth - this is a *process*. The fact that *Finding Your Way* is a process implies that you will be frustrated at times. Why? Because you cannot see the valley floor of your life accurately until you climb the mountain of self-discovery. Don't let this reality discourage you. There will be times when you will want to quit because you will feel confused. Don't quit. You might feel like you are trying to look out a steam coated window. Keep wiping the fog away one discovery at a time. You will complete a section and that will wipe some of the haze away but you still won't see yourself fully. Get used to it. Your friends may ask you if you've found your way yet and you will have to say to them, *"I'm doing the work, but it's just to early to tell."* That response might be worth memorizing.

If you have already read the *Finding Your Way* fable, you will recall Mark Johnson's reaction to the process. At times he thought he was crazy for continuing. But, he stayed with the process and it paid off. It will for you too. Just like Mark, you will *Look Back, Look In, Look Up* and *Look Out*. And just like Mark, you will be better in the end, more ready for your future.

The *FYWJ* is **best done in relationship with others**. You will be asked to seek the insights of others throughout this life discovery guide. The input and insights of friends and family will be critical to the success of the process. If you are working though this journal in the context of a class at a high school or university, a book club, a community education class or in a small group at church, you already have a built-in network of friends. This will be of great benefit. If you are doing the journal alone, invite some friends to go through this process with you. Start a group and do it together.

The *FYWJ* will **challenge you to trust your instincts**. You will be nudged (actually, pushed pretty hard) to listen closely to your inner thoughts and reactions to life. Trust what you hear. Trust what you feel. Don't compare yourself with others. This is about *your* life, not someone else's life. At the end of the process, one of the goals is that you will have paid close attention to yourself and better learned how to read from the pages of your life. This journal will become your personalized record of the insights you glean as you *Look Back, Look In, Look Up* and *Look Out*.

How the Journal will work for you -

The *FYWJ* has six sections. *Beginnings, Look Back, Look In, Look Up, Look Out* and *Wrapping It All Up.* Each section will build upon the other.

In each section you will . . .
    • reread a portion of the *Finding Your Way* fable engaging Mark Johnson as he attempts to find his way.
    • take time to consider important clarifying questions. If you are doing this journal with a group, you will discuss these together. The questions will move you from Mark Johnson's story to your own story.
    • take action and do some discovery assignments in the form of exercises. There will be plenty of space for you to record your findings.
    • think more about what this process is revealing about you. The homework will personalize the lessons for you.

Beginnings

GETTING STARTED

Mark Johnson finds himself in a very real and frustrating life situation. Before you interact with the questions below, read or reread these chapters at the beginning of the *Finding Your Way* book: *The Conversation, The Drive Back, The Wake Up and Caramel Latte (pages 15-30 - *note: if you are reading Finding Your Way in an e-Book format you won't find page numbers, so reference the chapter titles).*

Record your reaction to the emerging story of Mark Johnson.

1. What words would you use to describe Mark's current state of mind?

2. At the beginning of the story Mark isn't sure where he is headed and he is confused concerning his future. As you look at your future, where do you think you might be headed?

3. Do any of the words you used to describe Mark describe you? Which ones? Circle the words in question #1 that describe you. Write the three that most describe you below.

4. Does your answer to question #2 square with:

    a. Your parents' thoughts for you?

    b. Your close friends' thoughts of you?

5. What expectations did your mom and dad have placed _on them_ as they grew up? If you don't know, ask them.

6. As you enter the _Finding Your Way_ process, how do you feel? Mark had fears and hesitations, do you?

7. It seems like Mark's grandfather enjoyed Mark for simply being "Mark" with few expectations (pages 19-20 in *The Drive Back* chapter in *Finding Your Way*). Do you have people in your life that you are drawn to who seem to accept you for who you are? Who are they?

People who accept me for who I am:

8. Katie and Jim Clarke were willing to help Mark find his way. They were on his team. Who is on your team as you begin this process?

The people who are on my team:

As you begin the *Finding Your Way* process, how would you answer this?

I need to think more about . . .

Step One

 **LOOK BACK**

Theme: *"Look back before you look forward."*

Focus: *Look for clues that point to who you really are.*

Jim Clarke reveals to Mark that the first step to finding his way was to *Look Back*. Take a few minutes and read or reread the *Look Back* section in the *Finding Your Way* book which includes *Lemonade, The List, Cartoons and Cathedrals, Uncle Chuck* and *Calling Home (pages 32-47)*.

Before you were ten...
Many researchers believe that we are most truly ourselves when we are young. Compared to adults, children are more authentic and true to their honest emotions and reactions. Kids seem to reveal their genuine 'down deep' person in the years before they turn ten. This means that during your pre-ten years there are 'tells' concerning who you are at your core that can be discovered by spending time reflecting. This isn't the entire ball game, but it gives you a starting point.

Remember back through your school experiences.

Elementary school . . . we tend to most be ourselves. We live more on the surface of life expressing honest reactions and feelings.

Middle school . . . an explosion of insecurity chokes us. Our bodies begin to change. Our understanding of ourselves starts to change. For most of us the middle school years are difficult and painful.

High school . . . the monster of comparison rises up and works to blind us to who we truly are. During these years most of us measure ourselves in relation to those around us. We compare ourselves in the areas of talent, looks or intelligence. Doing this derails us. Rather than narrow in on our strengths and celebrate them, we get side-tracked wishing we were someone else. We discover there are certain people, certain looks and certain beliefs that are cooler than others. In those moments we are tempted to abandon our true selves and play a role. During this time we often forget who we are, and what we believe, just so we can fit in. When we do this, it sprays steam on the mirror and hinders our ability to see a true reflection of ourselves. Maybe you got lost during those days. Just think of all the opinionated voices that tried to get into your head and tell you who you were - friends who liked you, people who didn't like you, parents, church leaders, and all the other voices of the cultural you lived in. The following exercises will help you remember back to who you were during the single digit years of your life.

To Do #1 - Collecting thoughts about you

Mark identifies his mom, Mrs. Bush, and Uncle Chuck as the people who knew him before he was ten. Make a list below of those who knew you before you were ten years old. Give each person a call (or visit them personally) and ask them to identify some characteristics that were true of you when you were younger. If at all possible one of the three should to be one of your parents. Really listen to their thoughts. Brainstorm possible names below and record what they share with you on the next page.

Who can I ask?   *Contact Info:*

- _____   [_____]

- _____   [_____]

- _____   [_____]

- _____   [_____]

- _____   [_____]

- _____   [_____]

- _____   [_____]

"BEFORE I CAN TELL MY LIFE WHAT I WANT TO DO WITH IT.

To Do #2 - Creating your list

Make a list based on the conversations you had with those who knew you before age ten.

What was true about me before age ten:

Who I talked to: *What they said:*

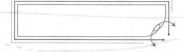

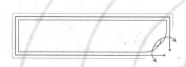

To Do #3 - Remembering how you played

Something else worth remembering is what you liked to do during play times when you were young. Think back - what did you enjoy doing? *Did you like to read alone in your room? Did you get on your bike and explore? Did you build things? Color and draw? Did you entertain people with your singing or acting? Were you the life of the party or quiet? Did you like to play with others or alone?* Allow these questions to stir your memory and write what you remember below.

What if...

What if your life before ten wasn't so rosy? What if you grew up in a home where those who raised you were disinterested, abusive or absent? What if your childhood memories are filled with pain? What if you don't even know who your parents are? What if you look back and all you feel is anger and sadness for what was taken from you during those early years? If that's you, I'm so sorry for the hurt you have experienced. My encouragement to you is to look the ugly truth of those days in the face acknowledging both the pain and sadness. Cry if you must. Talk with those you trust about your experiences and feelings. **Make a decision today to not allow the hurt of those days to own your future.** *You can rise up and move ahead. Consider reading stories about successful people who had tough upbringings but overcame them to live meaningful lives. Some of those stories can be read at the www.findingyourway.us website. Bottom line, the early days are just one chapter of your life and your whole future is ahead of you. The next three sections will offer lots of hope and insight as you move ahead to find your way.*

To Do #4 - EXTRA CREDIT...Photos of you

Here's an activity to confirm some of the insights you just learned about yourself before age ten. If you have access to photos of you before age ten, get them out or bring them up on a computer screen. With the list of characteristics from the previous pages in mind, look at the photos and see if any of them reveal insights as to who you were before age ten. Maybe someone reminded you that you were adventurous when you were young. Look for photos that would confirm that. Maybe you loved books. Any photos of you reading? Maybe you loved to build things or draw like Mark Johnson. Any pictures of you constructing or drawing? You get the point. Create a simple visual presentation of these as a way of creating a personal history of *'you.'*

Photos   **What they say about me?**

Tape
Photos
here

Write on
back of
photos...

what they
say about
you

To Do #5 - Genetics and DNA

There is something to say about strengths, talents and even passions being handed down from one generation to another through genetics. See what you can find out about your parents and grandparents strengths, talents and passions. Don't focus on who they WEREN'T, focus on their positive qualities. List them on the chart below and see if any of their strengths, talents or passions have been passed down in your DNA.

On the lines below record your parents and grandparents strengths, talents or passions.

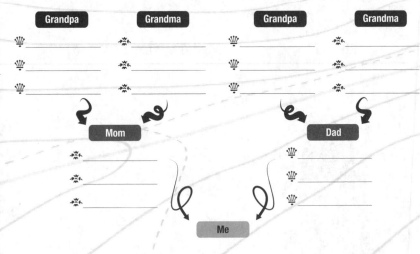

What strengths, talents or passions do I have that were (or are) in my parents or grandparents?

*(Go to page 172 and read about the "**What Others Say**" assignment. Start now collecting the 'upside' truth about you as you work through the journal. Don't wait until the end to do this assignment.)*

Step Two

 **LOOK IN**

Theme: *"Self-awareness is all about looking in."*

Focus: *Reactions reveal. Learning to read from the pages of our life experiences. What has caused you to react?*

Jim Clarke next helps Mark Johnson by directing him to *Look In*. Self-awareness is the lesson Mark must learn. To get going with this section read or reread the *Look In* chapters - *Frequencies, Think Time, Pizza, & Talking To Mom (pages 50-73)* of Mark's story in *Finding Your Way*.

To Do #1 - Your genuine interests in school

Make a list of classes you have taken. List the ones you enjoyed and the ones you didn't.

Favorite Classes	*Snooze-o marooz-o Classes*
• _____	_____
• _____	_____
• _____	_____
• _____	_____
• _____	_____
• _____	_____
• _____	_____
• _____	_____

What do these lists tell you about you and your interests?

To Do #2 - Your genuine interests at work

Think about the part or full time jobs you have had that you enjoyed. What did you like about each job? Maybe you only enjoyed fifty-percent of the job. Record what you liked about it.

Enjoyable Jobs	*What I liked about this job?*
• _____	_____
• _____	_____
• _____	_____
• _____	_____
• _____	_____
• _____	_____
• _____	_____
• _____	_____
• _____	_____

Now, think about the part or full time jobs you have had that you did NOT enjoy. What didn't you like about each job?

Hurry Up Friday Jobs	Why I didn't like this job?
• _____	_____
• _____	_____
• _____	_____
• _____	_____
• _____	_____
• _____	_____
• _____	_____
• _____	_____

What does this tell you about you and your interests?

To Do #3 - Your genuine interests as a volunteer

Think of any volunteer work you have done. Were any of these volunteer opportunities meaningful? Why?

Where I volunteered: *Why did I volunteer there?*   *What did I like about the experience?*

• _____ [_____] _____

_____

• _____ [_____] _____

_____

• _____ [_____] _____

_____

What does this tell you about you and your interests?

"The Big-Bad List About Me"

Take some time and make a list of what **To Do's #1-3** in this section say about you. Mark Johnson's list is at the end of the *Think Time* chapter (pages 62-63 in *Finding Your Way*). If you need some help reread his thoughts about himself.

- _____
- _____
- _____
- _____
- _____
- _____
- _____
- _____
- _____
- _____
- _____
- _____
- _____
- _____
- _____
- _____
- _____

- _____
- _____
- _____
- _____
- _____
- _____
- _____
- _____
- _____
- _____
- _____
- _____
- _____
- _____
- _____
- _____
- _____
- _____
- _____
- _____
- _____

To Do #4 - Pony up for Pizza

Mark Johnson invited Katie, Justin and Sara out for pizza and asked for their input in his process. Who will be part of that time for you? Invite three or four of your closest friends out to a meal or coffee and share with them your findings.

Who will you invite?

'Pizza dinner' findings...

What I learned from my friends at the 'pizza dinner'...

'Pizza dinner' findings continued . . .

To Do #5 - Create Your Passion List

What are your passions? Passions are about what you love.
These are things you can't get enough of. When you do them,
time flies by. You love to read about, be around, and learn about
your passions. From the reflection you have already done on the
previous pages, which of your passions have come to light? List
them below.

Define 'passion' in your own words . . .

I have a passion for:

_____

_____

_____

_____

_____

_____

_____

*(Go to page 172 and reread the "**What Others Say**" assignment.
Continue getting others input concerning the 'upside' truth about
you as you work through the journal. Don't wait until the end to
complete this assignment.)*

Step Three

LOOK UP

Theme: *"Recognize both the value of life, and the responsibility we each have, to positively contribute as human beings sharing this wonderful planet."*

Focus: *You have a responsibility to use the gifts and talents you were given.*

Jim Clarke invited a friend to help Mark understand the *Look Up* aspect of the *Finding Your Way process*. Remind yourself of the core lessons Jim wanted Mark to learn by reading or rereading the *Rev & First National Bank (pages 76-92)* chapters in *Finding Your Way*.

To Do #1 - Birth stories

If possible, ask one or both of your parents to share the story of your birth. Record your findings on the next page.

Another WHAT IF . . .

What if your parents are unavailable to share the story of your birth? It is possible you were abandoned or given up for adoption by your birth parents. Or perhaps your parents are simply not whole or healthy or mature enough to share it with you? Maybe they are just too darn busy to even care. You have a choice to make in regards to hurtful life experiences. You can stay focused, angry and bitter about what your parents didn't do for you, or you can remind yourself that your value is bigger than parents who simply dropped the ball when it came to caring for you.

Here's something you can do that will help remind you of what is most true about you - *that you have incredible value!* Identify two couples who have recently had a new baby. Maybe it's a friend, teacher or a neighbor or someone you know at church. Ask them to tell you about the birth of their new child and what they felt when the child was born. Really listen for their excitement.

What words did they use to describe the experience? How would you describe their attitude towards their new child?

Their excited reaction is what every child needs to hear over and over from his or her parents. It communicates value to the child. Please remember, if you aren't able to hear your parents tell you your birth story - it DOESN'T MEAN YOU DON'T HAVE VALUE. *You do!*

What do these birth stories, either your own or someone else's, remind you about the value of every human life?

To Do #2 - World view and personal faith

The *Finding Your Way* book, and this journal, is not specifically about religious beliefs or world views. But to be honest, it is difficult to talk about your life purpose and not provide some space in this journal where you can think about this issue and consider your beliefs. Think seriously about the following question:

How does what you believe (your view of life and the world . . . or your personal faith) influence your thoughts about the value of your life and future?

This is not a simple question, but those who find their way answer it sooner of later. It is simply a question that every person must think about sometime during his or her life. If you are working through the *FYWJ* with others *be sure to listen and respect each group member's personal beliefs* when you discuss this question.

How does my world view or personal faith influence how I see my value and future?

_____

_____

_____

_____

_____

_____

_____

_____

_____

To Do #3 - How others got there

Identify two people you know who live with a *'Look Up'* attitude. These are people who show up every day and joyfully use their talents for the good of the world.

Identify two people: _____

_____

Here are three questions to ask them . . .

First Q - *"Over the time I've known you, I have noticed something true about you. You seem to be happy in life. You show up everyday with joy and generously share your talents and gifts for the good of the world around you. Why do you do that? and . . . How do you pull it off day after day?"*

_____'s response . . .

_____'s response . . .

Second Q - *"How did you find your way to your life contribution? What was that process like for you?"*

_____'s response . . .

_____'s response . . .

Third Q - *"What role has your world view (or personal faith) played in helping you find your way to your life contribution?"*

_____'s response . . .

_____'s response . . .

Take a few minutes and summarize your 'Look Up' learnings.

_____

_____

_____

_____

_____

_____

_____

_____

_____

_____

_____

_____

_____

_____

_____

_____

_____

_____

(Go to page 172 and reread the "What Others Say" assignment. Continue getting others input concerning the 'upside' truth about you as you work through the journal. Don't wait until the end to complete this assignment.)

Step Four

LOOK OUT

Theme: *"The application of you in the real world."*

Focus: *Aligning yourself with a specific vocation and finding your sweet spot.*

In the last section of *Finding Your Way,* Jim Clarke helps Mark Johnson think about the application of his life in the real world. As you begin this section read or reread the *Look Out* chapters in *Finding Your Way* - *Regents, An Outrageous Opportunity, The Call, One Last Latte, Mark's Letter, Graduation, and Epilogue (pages 94-118).*

To Do #1 - Your Matrix

It's time for you to fill in the *Finding Your Way Matrix* (there is an extra matrix on pages 162). *Down the left side* of the matrix record the statements that you have discovered are true about you. Use the information you've gleaned from the exercises: child-hood interviews, self-awareness insights and reactions, classes liked and disliked, jobs liked and disliked, insights from friends. *Across the top* of the matrix on the slanted lines write vocational (or educational) options that both make sense and excite you.

Here are two suggestions if you are having trouble and need a jump-start: *First,* take a look at Mark's Matrix on page 102 in *Finding Your Way. Second,* find a mentor to talk with. This might be a guidance counselor (both high schools and colleges have these) or someone you sense has an interest in helping people sort themselves out. Maybe you could find and talk with a director of human resources from a local company.

Finding Your Way Matrix

Across the top write vocational or educational options that excite you.

Record statements below that are true about you that need to be present in your vocation.

Inside the grid boxes above put a **"yes"** if the statement about you in the left column would be true in the vocation, **"no"** if it would not be true, and **a "question mark"** if you aren't sure. Then consider what the **yes's**, **no's** and **question marks** mean.

Finding Your Way Matrix

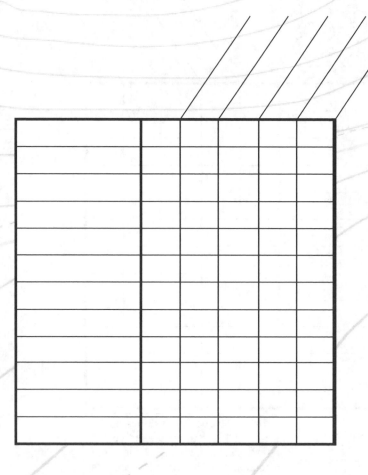

To Do #2 - Assessing Your Matrix

Inside the grid boxes to the right of the statements that are true about you, put a *"yes"* in each box if it would make the statement about you on the left true, *"no"* if it would not. Place a "*question mark"* if your aren't sure.

Where are the most 'yes' answers?

What do these answers reveal about you and your future?

To Do #3 - Write the letter

Jim Clarke gave Mark Johnson one final assignment. Take a minute and read about it on page 113 in *Finding Your Way*. The assignment was for Mark to write a letter to his dad explaining what he had learned through the *Finding Your Way Process*. The letter summarized Mark's learning as he *Looked Back, Looked In, Looked Up* and *Looked Out*. The letter gave his dad a glimpse into both the *process* and the *progress* Mark had made in understanding himself and his future.

You may write your letter to a parent or someone who has walked with you through this process. Maybe you will simply read it to your small group or class. But it is important to write it and summarize what you've learned for yourself and those who read it.

For whom will you write your letter?

TO:

My Letter

My Letter continued

" . . . BECAUSE TALENT ISN'T GENIUS, AND NO AMOUNT OF ENERGY CAN MAKE IT SO . . .

I WANT TO BE GREAT, OR NOTHING." LOUISA MAY ALCOTT - LITTLE WOMEN

Who did you share your letter with and what was their reaction?

_____

_____

_____

_____

_____

_____

_____

_____

_____

_____

_____

_____

_____

_____

_____

_____

Wrapping it up . . .

Congratulations!

You have almost completed the *Finding Your Way Process*. While this is a great accomplishment, it's only the beginning of the rest of your life. Now it's important to ask, *"What are the right next steps for me to take to insure I live the life I am meant to live?"*

Here are some thoughts on how to do this:

1. Be sure to write and share your 'what I've learned through this process' letter. This exercise is important because it allows you to review the key truths you learned about yourself through the process. It will also be meaningful for those who have walked through the process with you to hear your thoughts, insights, and learnings.

2. Create an ACTION PLAN.
Think through the next 'right steps' for you to take to move ahead. In your ACTION PLAN on the next page record -

> *a. What are the next right steps to take?*
>
> *b. What specific help will I need?*
>
> *c. Who can offer me that help?*

As you move into your future you will need the support and encouragement of others. Identify who those people are. Write their names on the next page and determine what you will need from them. If you are a student, your next action might be to further investigate majors of interest. If you are already in the work world, hopefully you have greater clarity for your next vocational choice. If you are currently looking for your next job, the findings should point you in the right direction. Wherever you find yourself, there are right ACTION STEPS that you will want to identify as you complete this process. Write those down now.

MY ACTION PLAN -

1 • *Next right step:* _____

• *What help will I need?* _____

• *Who can help?* _____

2 • *Next right step:* _____

• *What help will I need?* _____

• *Who can help?* _____

3 • *Next right step:* _____

• *What help will I need?* _____

• *Who can help?* _____

4 • *Next right step:* _____

• *What help will I need?* _____

• *Who can help?* _____

5 • *Next right step:* _____

• *What help will I need?* _____

• *Who can help?* _____

3. Consider becoming a Jim Clarke to someone who is trying to find his or her way. Do you know anyone who would benefit from this process? Why not share the book and process with them. The *Finding Your Way* movement offers training that will equip you to help others find their way. If you are a parent, coach, teacher, spiritual guide, friend, relative or just someone who cares, *Finding Your Way* can be a wonderful gift to those searching for a clear path. More information is available at www.findingyourway.us.

Who do I know that needs this process?

Names:

PARTICULAR THING IN IT. AND IT'S VERY HARD FOR PEOPLE TO STOP YOU." BILL COSBY, COMEDIAN

What Others Say

. . . discovering the truth about you

Who currently are the most supportive people in your life? These are the people who know you best and genuinely love you. Are they friends? Relatives? Teachers? Coaches? Spiritual leaders? Work associates? Do you have any idea what these caring people consider to be your strengths, talents and positive characteristics? It's time for you to find out by asking them for their thoughts.

Before you invite them to identify the *upside truth* about you, make a list of those who know you and sincerely care about you.

- _____
- _____
- _____
- _____
- _____
- _____
- _____
- _____
- _____

Final Task - Collecting the 'Upside Truth' About You

CAUTION - This assignment is risky. Why? Because you are going to ask a number of friends (those whose names you just wrote down on your list) to tell you in written form their perception of the **upside truth** about you. You may think, *"You have to be kidding? They won't want to do that."* Or you may think, *"No one will have anything nice to say."* Trust me, you will be surprised at what people will say. Remember, you are inviting the thoughts of people who know you, care about you, and want to see you succeed. What they write on the following pages will be a treasure that you can come back to and read over and over again.

Ready? Here's what to do next . . .

First - look at the next few pages. You'll notice that there is room for a number of different people to write positive thoughts about you. They will each have a couple pages to record their thoughts.

Second - identify from the list on the previous page the people you will invite to share their perspective concerning the truth about you.

Third - take this book/journal and give it to each person for a short time. Ask them to share in written form on the following pages their perspective concerning your strengths and positive characteristics. Let them know that what they write doesn't need to be long. They can write a few paragraphs or simply list some bullet points. Emphasize to them that it is important that they be sincere. Remind them that you only want POSITIVE input and ask them to take this seriously.

What Others Say

. . . discovering the truth about you

#1 -

_____ thoughts concerning the truth about me.
_{name}

What Others Say

. . . discovering the truth about you

#2 -

_____ *thoughts concerning the truth about me.*

name

What Others Say

. . . discovering the truth about you

#3 -

_____ thoughts concerning the truth about me.
name

What Others Say
. . . discovering the truth about you

#4 -

_____ *thoughts concerning the truth about me.*
name

ALI
i2i

About the Authors

Dan Webster is a life long student, practitioner and pioneer in the area of leadership and life development. He has worked with numerous senior leaders across multiple sectors in the for-profit, non-profit, para-church, educational and church worlds. Dan served on the staff of two influential churches where he had the opportunity to build two of the largest and most effective student ministries in America. He has also been a distinguished visiting scholar in the Values-Driven Leadership PhD/D.B.A. program at Benedictine University in Chicago.

In 1995 he founded *Authentic Leadership, Inc.* Since then he has devoted his life to speaking, writing, and mentoring leaders inside and outside the church. He has written numerous books. His latest, *KidUnique: Helping Kids Discover Who They Are*, empowers concerned adults to build discovery rich relationships with those who are young. Dan regularly inspires those older to take greater interest in young people through his KidUnqiue workshop.

As a communicator and mentor, Dan has presented on numerous occasions at conferences and events in South America, Europe, Canada and all across the United States. Among the wide variety of topics he addresses are - becoming an authentic leader, transformational leadership, the six phases of leader development, leading from the pages of your life, upside-down leadership, situational parenting, how to help kids discover who they are, and increasing your personal impact. His audiences enjoy his honesty, authenticity and sense of humor. His messages hit the head and the heart with practical steps that move the listener toward the life they are meant to live.

Dan and his wife Judy live in Holland, MI. They have three grown sons, Luke, Landan and Logan.

Randy Gravitt has invested his life in helping people grow. His passion is to help next generation leaders understand the importance of living a life of integrity in order to maximize their influence. He has worked in education, both as a teacher and coach, served over a decade on the staff of one of the largest churches in the Atlanta area, and been a public speaker and writer. In 2009, Randy founded Randy Gravitt Leadership, where he encourages leaders to remain character based through his speaking and writing. He has mentored dozens of leaders through personal coaching. Randy writes a daily leadership blog at randygravitt.com and can be followed on twitter at twitter.com/randygravitt.

Randy has written *Character for Kids, 30 Days to a More Godly Man,* and *30 Days to Financial Focus.* He enjoys teaching on the topics of leadership, marriage and family, and health and fitness.

As a communicator, Randy has spoken to hundreds of audiences around the world. He has taught in the U.S., Europe, Asia, Africa, and South America. Randy has presented to corporations such as Chick-fil-A, as well as Fellowship of Christian Athletes, college and professional sports teams, and taught life and leadership skills in both private and public schools across the country. His audiences are drawn to his encouragement and motivational style of speaking aimed at bringing about transformation.

Randy enjoys marathon and trail running, reading, traveling, and serving as a community coach for various sports teams in his local area.

He and his wife Laura live in Sharpsburg, Georgia. They have four daughters, Hannah, Sarah, Rebekah, and Katherine.

Acknowledgements

Special thanks go out to...

* Denny and Scoob Ellens who always have interest and energy for the next idea. Their generosity, time and friendship in many ways make what I do possible.
* Dave and Lori Chow. Dave's relentless hunger to grow, understand truth and serve wholeheartedly inspires me. He is the pupil who has become the teacher.
* Gus Gustafson is the smartest and most positive person I know. His passion to see every person on the planet become a super-charged socially responsible leader keeps me focused.
* Brian and Mary Lubinski. Brian, more than any other person, reminds me that my life matters. It takes a 'best friend' to pull that off.
* Linda Lindquist-Bishop for modeling what it is to live an extraordinary life and cheering others to do the same.
* The Benedictine University Ph.D./D.B.A. cohort who generously shared their time and collective intellect vetting this project. Greg, be sure to keep the wild bunch under control.
* Terry Schulenburg. Terry is brilliant, an awesome dad and husband, and an amazing friend who has cared about the work of *Authentic Leadership, Inc.* since it's inception. He is also an incredible mentor to young men. He led his small group of ten high school seniors through *Finding Your Way.* The results of that small group changed the game concerning this project.
* Terry's *So Cal Bad Boyz Small Group.* You guys rock and each have incredible futures. Thanks to Andrew Archer, Jon Bixby, Chris Diaz, Matthew French, Cody Garrison, Tyler Hadley, James Helman, Austin Schulenburg, Sean Taylor and Zachary Zamora.
* Janice Rutledge, our editor, who believed in this project from the get-go. Her gifts have done what Randy and I could not do.
* Rohn Ritzema. His first class mind and educational instincts helped so much in creating the rubric and the educational application of the project.
* Judy Webster. My wife, love, companion and life-partner.
* My sons - Luke, Landan and Logan. To see each of them touch the world from their gifts and talents makes all the effort of helping each find his way worth it.
* All the generous people who took the time to read the manuscript and offer their insights and suggestions...thanks for caring.
* God, who has patiently and lovingly used so many people over the years to help me find my way. To honor God in all I do is life indeed.

- Dan Webster, March 2014

The list is endless of those who have encouraged me to Find My *own* Way and to write this book.

* My wife Laura is such an incredible gift. She continues to be the best thing in my life and my best friend.
* To my four beautiful and unique daughters, Hannah, Sarah, Rebekah, and Katherine, you girls are my favorite part of every day. Watching you discover why God put you on the planet is awesome. I am cheering for you to *Find Your Way*, maximize your influence, and to bring Him glory.
* My parents, who encouraged me that I could be anything I set my mind and heart to, deserve more than a simple thank you. Their wisdom encouraged me toward the right path.
* Ryan and Ronna, I love watching you and your families make a difference in the world. You are the two best educators I have ever known, and it is an honor to have you call me Big Bro.
* My friend Mark Miller encouraged me to consider a fable, and my brothers from the *Real Deal* group prayed for me and gave great feedback on the initial draft. You guys have helped me go to the next level as a leader.
* Special thanks to the dozen friends who gave their input to the manuscript. They came armed with red pens and some awesome suggestions. Thank you all.
* I am privileged to work with some of the most selfless people on earth. Thanks to the entire CRC team, and a special shout out to Russell Brown, aka the Bear, and to John Orr who shares his reading list with me.
* Janice Rutledge and her insightful review were awesome.
* Philip and Lorri Swords, who gave me the opportunity to practice the Life Planning process, deserve a huge thank you.
* To all the students I have had the blessing of teaching, coaching, and learning alongside over the past several years. The future is bright!
* Thanks to the Landmark Leadership Academy for allowing me to present the *Finding Your Way* module.
* Finally, praise be to God for the gift of life and for reminding us all, "*. . . we are fearfully and wonderfully made.*" My desire is to bring Him honor as I seek to live a life of integrity and influence.

- Randy Gravitt - March 2014

Additional Resources

Dan Webster

kidunique: *Helping Kids Discover Who They Are*

Be an adult who makes a
difference in the life of a young person.

Young people have an innate need for adults who will cheer for them, see the best in them and support them through both words and deeds. **kid**unique is all about preparing you as an adult to fulfill that essential role in the life of a young person. This task may sound intimidating, but **kid**unique skillfully guides you from a passive position into an active role in a young person's life through the **"four-window model"** of **observation, exploration, affirmation,** and **revelation**. Find out about **kid**unique and the **kid**unique workshop at www.kidunique.com.

Softcover, 196 pages, ISBN 978-0-7644-6682-3

KIDS.
OUR FUTURE IS DEPENDING ON THEM.

Everyone says that, but you mean it.
You are doing something to help.

Be part of kidunque
and unexpected things happen.
You inspire a kid to make the contribution
they were born to make.
You help a kid to live an extraordinary life.
You brighten the future.

Be part of kidunque
and change the world --
one kid at a time.

Host a WORKSHOP

Dan Webster and Randy Gravitt travel the country creatively sharing the *finding your way* process through their **Finding Your Way Workshop**.

At the workshop each attendee will:
- learn in detail the *Finding Your Way* process from the authors
- personalize the process through an experiential learning environment
- complete a matrix identifying vocational options
- walk away with practical action steps to move into the future

Investigate the possibilities for your school, community organization, business or church at **www.findingyourway.us**.

• • • • •

Speaking Engagements

Contact information for booking either of the authors to present at your organization, school or church.

Dan Webster
Founder
Authentic Leadership, Inc.
550 Old Orchard Road
Holland, MI   49423
dan@authenticleadershipinc.com
www.authenticleadershipinc.com

Randy Gravitt
Founder
Randy Gravitt Leadership
45 Hazelridge Lane
Sharpsburg, GA   30277
randy@randygravitt.com
www.randygravitt.com

Check out the online version of the

Finding Your Way
Book and **Journal**

at

www.fywjournal.com

The *Finding Your Way Journal* website serves teachers, leaders, and students in educational institutions, as well as individuals, who want to experience the online version of the *Finding Your Way* process.

Bring **FINDING YOUR WAY** to your community

We are CRAZY about young people
and we bet you are too!

For the next generation to reach their potential they need someone who is CRAZY about them.

Who are YOU crazy about?

Maybe it's a young person . . .
- in your own family
- in the class you teach
- on a sports team you coach
- who works for you
- in your youth group at church or synagogue
- in your neighborhood.

EVERY young person needs someone they can look up to who sincerely cares about them. You can help the next generation discover **how great they are, how gifted they are,** and **how bright a future they can have.**

HOW?

We have a dream of communities all around the world launching a movement of young people who have discovered their purpose for living. Imagine what could happen if every graduating senior at your local high school experienced the *FINDING YOUR WAY process.* Let's work together to make that happen.

Dan Webster & Randy Gravitt

Join the cause at
www.findingyourway.us